1 MONTH OF
FREE
READING

at

www.ForgottenBooks.com

By purchasing this book you are eligible for one month membership to ForgottenBooks.com, giving you unlimited access to our entire collection of over 1,000,000 titles via our web site and mobile apps.

To claim your free month visit: www.forgottenbooks.com/free1124719

ISBN 978-0-331-44343-1
PIBN 11124719

BOSTON UNIVERSITY

College of Business Administration

THESIS

The Historical Development of Chain Stores

by

Philip Thomas Egan, Jr.

(A. B. Holy Cross College 1936)

submitted in partial fulfillment of
the requirements for the degree of

MASTER OF BUSINESS ADMINISTRATION

1938

INTRODUCTION

One of the most interesting studies in the field of distribution is the development of the chain store. This subject has always been a bone of contention between chain store defenders and adversaries.

It is my purpose to present the historical development of the chain store and try to explain its growth from the time of its origin to its present state of development.

In preparing this thesis, I have procured the data from the most recent and reliable sources known to me. The material presented here has not been selected with the ultimate purpose of defending any conclusion previously formulated, but instead was chosen with the intention of giving an accurate account of the chain store situation, and from the data assembled arriving at an unprejudiced conclusion.

As far as I know, the sources of authority from which I have received my information are unbiased accounts that present the facts with no attempt to deceive or mislead.

It is from these sources that I shall trace the development of the chain store system, explain its problems, and arrive at a conclusion based on fact rather than on prejudice.

TABLE OF CONTENTS

DEFINITION OF CHAIN STORES

At least one of the reasons for the chain store controversy can be found in a misunderstanding of the essence of the chain store problem. Some of this misapprehension, in turn, can be laid to crass ignorance of the most rudimentary concepts inherent in the question. There is complete lack of knowledge even among the intelligent laymen of what a chain store is and of how one class of chains differs from another, let alone the significance of the economic, social, and political problems to which chain stores have given rise.

Unfortunately, much of this misunderstanding has developed from attempts **made** by writers on the subject and so-called "researchers" to becloud the issue. Many of them very definitely seem to have had an axe to grind; others may have had a special purpose in mind to which they have fitted their concepts. For these reasons, it would seem fitting and proper at this juncture to define a few essential terms and to attempt to state the nature of the chain store problem. In this wise the scope of this discussion will be limited and a clear understanding will be had of the fundamental questions involved.

WHAT IS A CHAIN?--A considerable part of the difficulty to which we have alluded in the preceding paragraphs can be attributed to the confusion among the terms "chain store," "chain," and "chain system." Some authors have apparently

attempted to define one or another of these terms without
giving the slightest indication of their effort, and, perhaps, without themselves being aware of the confusion in
their own minds. That may explain in part some of the differences in definitions of chains to be found in the liter-
ature on the subject. Then there is the obvious attempt to
understate or over-emphasize the importance of chains in our
distribution system, depending upon the objective to be ac-
complished. Moreover, the whole subject has very often been
conceived so narrowly as to confine the term chain to retail
distributive operations. Thus, although we are all familiar
with certain kinds of chain stores and chain systems, the
concept of what is a chain has never been adequately defined.

Among the most important factors to be considered in
defining a chain are: the number of units in the organization, the type of merchandise handled or the kind of business,
the plane of operation, the degree of central ownership, and
the extent of centralized management. In its investigation
of chain stores, the Federal Trade Commission has defined the
term "chain" or "chain store" as "an organization owning a
controlling interest in two or more establishments which sell
substantially similar merchandise at retail." In its definition the Commission uses two units as the point of departure
from independent stores, confines the term to the retail

field, emphasizes the idea of centralized ownership, lays down as a prerequisite the carrying of substantially similar lines of merchandise by the various units of the chain, and disregards any reference to centralized management. The other official definition of the term is that used by the various units of the chain, and disregards any reference to centralized management. The other official definition of the term is that used by the Bureau of the Census in connection with its censuses of retail distribution. In its publications, this Bureau states that "chains are groups of four or more stores in the same general kind of business, owned and operated jointly, with central buying, usually supplied from one or more central warehouses." On this basis, a chain is a group of four or more stores in the same kind or field of business, under the one ownership and management, and supplied from one or more distributing warehouses or directly from the manufacturer on orders placed by the central buying organization. Consequently, the two Federal agencies differ in their concepts of what is a chain in at least two important respects: the minimum number of units necessary to classify a retail organization as a chain, and the necessity for centralized management especially centralized buying. [1]

DEFINITION OF TERMS.--There is a difference of opinion as to the number of stores necessary to constitute a chain. The legislative bills of Mississippi and Indiana define a chain as two or more stores as do Hayward and White, Paul H.

Nystrom, and R. W. Lyons. The anti-chain measures introduced
in several states specify that there must be five or more u-
nits under common ownership and management before a chain exists. The United States Bureau of Census does not classify
a retail organization as a chain unless it has more than three
units. The Federal Trade Commission in its Inquiry tenta-
tively defined a chain store as an organization controlling
and operating two or more units.

1. "Two or more retail establishments operating under
common management, ownership or ultimate capital control
engaged in the sale of goods, wares, or merchandise."

> R. W. Lyons, Executive Vice-President, National
> Chain Store Association.

2. "A chain store consists of a number of unit stores
operating under common management and control, and following
common policies and utilizing common methods of operation
which are determined by the central management."

> Fred S. Clark, Professor of Marketing, Northwestern
> University.

3. "The chain store is a corporation engaged primarily
in retailing of merchandise through a fairly large number of
store units which are owned and controlled by the corporation."

> James L. Palmer, Associate Professor of Marketing,
> University of Chicago, from the Journal of Business,
> July, 1929, p. 272.

0

This technicality becomes of small importance in dealing with the vital issues of debate.

Chains classified as to types of operation and territory served.

1.   "A local chain"----"A local chain is a group of substantially similar stores under the same ownership and operation, merchandised from a central warehouse or other common point or points, but not from the stocks of a parent store. In a local chain, a majority of its stores are located in and around one city." [1]

2.   "A branch system"----"A branch system differs from a local chain, either of which can have four or more units, mainly in the method of merchandising and the relation of the various stores to each other. A branch system always revolves around a dominant parent store, which the branches grew from and from whose stocks the branches draw most of their merchandise for sale." [1]

3.   "A sectional chain"----"A sectional chain is one whose stores are located in a number of cities so that its interests are more than local, but a large majority of whose stores are located within one geographic division, or an equivalent area made up of parts of two geographic divisions."

[1] Beckman pp. 2-6

4.   "National chains"----"National chains are those
operating in two or more sections of the country whose
interests are too broad to be limited to any one section
of the country." [1]

"A voluntary Chain" is a group of retailers (each of
whom owns and operates his own store) either associated
with a wholesale grocer or acting cooperatively, organized
to carry on jointly merchandising activities and to combine
wholesale and retail functions under one control." [2]

The first of these classes is termed NATIONAL because
the companies included within its roster operate from coast-
to-coast. Outstanding among these NATIONAL companies are
such corporations as the F. W. Woolworth Company, the Great
Atlantic and Pacific Tea Company, the J. C. Penney Company,
Montgomery Ward and Company, Sear, Roebuck and Company,
Lerner Stores Company (apparel stores) and the retail stores
of the Goodyear, Firestone and Goodrich Tire and Rubber Companies. Each of the foregoing companies operates retail
establishments in forty or more states of the Union...from
the Atlantic to the Pacific Ocean and from the Great Lakes
to the Gulf of Mexico.

Sectional chain store companies are those which operate
stores in a number of communites, limited to individual

[1] Beckman pp. 2-6
[2] V. H. Pelz, Director of American Institute of Food Dis-
    tribution, Inc., from the Voluntary Chain, p. 5--Buehler 59-

sections of the country, such, for example, as in the New
England States or on the Pacific Coast or in the Gulf South-
west or in any other geographic division.

A typical example of this "sectional" type of chain
store is the Kroger Grocery and Baking Company which, though
operating approximately 4,238 stores in sixteen states, is,
nevertheless, not considered a national institution in the
strictest sense, since its trading activities are confined
primarily to the Middle Western states. By the same token,
the First National Stores, Incorporated (grocery) which confines its retailing activities almost entirely to the six
New England States, is certainly to be classed as a sectional
chain store company.

Chain store companies are classified as local if substantially all of their stores are located in but one community. By far the largest number of chain store companies
are local concerns. Among the better known ones are such
grocery corporations as the Thomas Roulston Company, H. C.
Bohack, Inc., and Daniel Reeves, Inc., all of New York City;
the Standard Grocery Company of Indianapolis, Indiana, the
National Grocery Company and the Mutual Grocery Company operating only in New Jersey; Autenreith's Variety Stores of
Pennsylvania and a score of others. [1]

[1] John P. Nichols pp. 9 and 10

CHAINS are groups of four or more stores in the same
general kind of business, owned and operated jointly, with
central buying, usually supplied from one or more central
warehouses. The count of units does not include the warehouses nor buying offices maintained apart from the stores.
Chains are local if substantially all of their stores are
located in and around some one city; sectional if in only
one part of the country; national if in more than one
section. [1]

The concentration of activity and geographic distribution of chain stores throughout the United States may be
seen by examining the following statistics:

The chain sales ratio is higher than the national
average of 22.8% in twelve states, as follows:

California	25.7%	Michigan	25.3%
Connecticut	24.5%	New Jersey	25.1%
District of Columbia	29.7%	New York	25.0%
Illinois	29.3%	Pennsylvania	24.9%
Indiana	24.3%	Rhode Island	26.2%
Massachusetts	28.9%	Ohio	24.0%

In all of these states the chain sales ratio was also
higher than the national average of 1929. [1]

[1] Census of Business: 1935

The twelve states with the lowest chain sales ratio
in 1935 are:

Mississippi	11.1%	North Dakota	15.9%
Arkansas	12.3%	New Mexico	15.9%
Wyoming	14.7%	South Carolina	16.2%
Montana	14.8%	Nebraska	16.5%
Minnesota	15.1%	Alabama	16.7%
Nevada	15.2%	Wisconsin	17.6%

Census of Business: 1935 p.8

II

ORIGIN OF CHAIN STORES

HISTORY OF THE CHAIN STORE--The chain store did not
spring up overnight like magic, as many people seem to
think. Its fundamental principle can clearly be traced
back at least four or five hundred years. Some of the best-
known older chain systems were found in England among the
Merchant Adventurers who operated under a Royal Charter.
Another prominent organization was the Fuggers of Augsburg,
Germany. This company or house engaged in both trading and
manufacturing. Still another well-known ancient system had
its origin in Japan and was called the Mitsui system. This
system originated as early as 1643 as a chain of apothecary
shops, and to this day it is still a powerful organization
in the drug business. All these giant organizations were
simply chain systems buying and selling under central control
and management much like the chains of today.

In this country the multi-unit system of distribution
goes back into our history before the Revolutionary War.
The Hudson Bay Company probably is the oldest chain in America. It was founded in 1670, and during the following dec-
ades established hundreds of trading posts which flourished
and prospered throughout the Colonial period. This company
still operates in the leading cities of Western Canada, where
it conducts wholesale establishments and fur trading posts.

ECONOMIC AND INDUSTRIAL REVOLUTION INFLUENCED CHAIN
GROWTH--Although chain systems of distribution have existed

in some form or another for hundreds of years, it required
the recent economic and industrial revolution to make possible the wholesale development of thousands of nation-wide
chain organizations as we know them today. None of the older
systems compared to our modern chains in the matter of efficiency of management and standardization of merchandise. Not
until the middle of the nineteenth century did we see the
origin of the efficiently managed chain store. It was during
the later fifties, before the Civil War, that a New York merchant, George Gilman, whose trade was none too brisk in his
hide-and-leather business, became provoked at the high prices
charged for tea and decided to set up a tea shop of his own.
Mr. Gilman, upon hearing that a shipload of tea lay unloaded
in the harbor for want of a buyer, immediately proceeded to
purchase the entire cargo. His new side-line required new
quarters; so he secured a small shop on Vesey Street, crudely
decorated the front of the store with red paint, stocked it
with tea, coffee, and spices, and placed in charge of it a
young man from Boston, George Huntington Hartford. It seems
that Hartford possessed a greater vision of the future than
his older partner, for he soon purchased Mr. Gilman's interests in the store and with prophetic vision organized "The
Great Atlantic and Pacific Tea Company," which has since become the largest single chain store company in the world with
an annual business of more than a billion dollars--an amount
exceeding the business done by the Great Pennsylvania
Railroad system.

Mr. Hartford's organization in 1865, which consisted of
twenty-five stores scattered over New York and Brooklyn, met
with mountains of difficulties through its slow expansion for
almost fifty years. In 1911 and 1912, The Great Atlantic and
Pacific Tea Company was struggling along with a few more than
four hundred stores, when it introduced the well-known "cash-
and-carry" system. In the following eighteen years this chain
increased its size almost thirty-five times, expanding from
four hundred and fifty stores in 1912, to more than fifteen
thousand in 1930. The business triumph of this largest, oldest, and best-known chain organization in the United States
comprises one of the most romantic stories in American mercantile history.

The key to young Hartford's business success lies in
the simple chain store principle of selling merchandise in
large amounts with a small margin of profit. This same principle has since proven the key to the successful development
of hundreds of other chain systems.

The next large chain organization was the Jones Brothers
Tea Company, founded in 1872. In 1928, this organization
changed its name and became the Grand Union Tea Company, under
which title it has since operated; at the present time it con-
trols more than thirteen hundred meat and grocery stores.

One of the most familiar of our modern chain stores is
commonly called the five and ten cent store. However, not
all of the five and ten cent chains sell merchandise exclu-
sively at the five and ten cent prices; many of them sell

articles ranging from five cents to one dollar. In the
years of business depression following the Civil War a five-
dollar-a-week clerk in the small town of Watertown, New York,
asked permission of the proprietor to collect a group of miscellaneous articles which for months and months had failed to
sell, and to place them all on one counter for sale at a nickel
each. These articles sold like marbles at a bargain counter
on the first warm spring day. The name of this five-dollar-a
week clerk was Frank W. Woolworth. The success of the five
cent sale encouraged young Woolworth to borrow capital and
go to Utica, where he set up the first five cent store. The
store failed, but Mr. Woolworth did not give up. He sold
half his stock for what money he could get, took the other
half and tried again in Lancaster, Pennsylvania, where he met
with fair success. Soon Woolworth joined the nickel and the
dime into partnership and opened other stores under the name
of "Woolworth's Five and Ten Cent Stores." Two years ago at
the Golden Jubilee, the fifty-year anniversary of the nickel
and dime union, the Woolworth concern controlled twenty-one
hundred stores, located in fifteen hundred cities in five
different countries, with annual sales amounting to nearly
three hundred million dollars.

III

DEVELOPMENT OF CHAIN STORES

OTHER CHAINS FOLLOW WOOLWORTH PLAN--Other chain stores
of the five and ten cent variety have successfully followed
the general plan of Mr. Woolworth. Included in this group is
J. G. McCrory, who began in 1882 with a capital of two thousand dollars and built up a chain of two hundred and forty-
five stores with total annual sales exceeding forty million
dollars. Out of Mr. McCrory's establishment another chain
of similar type originated. One of Mr. McCrory's early employees, S. S. Kresge, soon became his business partner.
Kresge remained with McCrory's until 1899, when he founded
the S. S. Kresge Company. This newly formed company sold
not only articles of the five and ten cent variety, but other
articles at twenty-five cents. The Kresge organization grew
by leaps and bounds, and today, although scarcely half as old
as Woolworth's organization, operated over five hundred stores,
doing a volume of business in excess of one hundred and fifty
million dollars. Another leading chain store in the five and
ten cent field is that of S. H. Kress and Company, established
in Memphis, Tennessee, in 1896, and today operating over two
hundred stores with annual sales of sixty-nine million dollars.

Although chain stores featuring articles from five to
ten cents seemed to be more familiar to the public before
1900 than other types of chains, there were formed other organizations which have since grown to national prominence.
Among these concerns are J. Butler Company, formed in 1882;

Hana & Sons Shoe Company, formed in 1885; Acme Tea Stores, formed in 1887; H. C. Bohack and Company, formed in 1887; New York and London Drug Company, formed in 1897; and the Jewel Tea Company, formed in 1899. Since 1900 a great number of chain organizations have come into existence. Space will permit mention of only the best-known concerns. Among these are the United Cigar Stores Company, formed in 1900; the J. C. Penney Company, formed in 1902; The United Drug Company formed in 1902; W. T. Grant Company, formed in 1906; Walgreen Company, formed in 1906; Louis K. Liggett Company, formed in 1907; McLellan Stores Company, formed in 1913; Safeway Stores, formed in 1914; and the Piggly Wiggly Corporation, formed in 1916.

THREE PERIODS IN CHAIN STORE DEVELOPMENT--As we look back over the history of the chain store, we may divide its development into three general periods. The first period may be called the pioneer period, dating from the birth of the Atlantic and Pacific Tea Company in 1858 and extending to 1900. The second Period may be called the period of development, dating from 1900 to the close of the World War. The third period may be called the period of growth and expansion, dating from 1918 to the present time.

1858-1900 During the pioneer period we witnessed the origin of many five and ten chains and a great number of tea companies, commonly known as food stores. The chains during this time met with many hardships and their expansion was very

slow. We should remember that nearly all of the organizations in this period developed from one single store. Through the skillful management of the owner of one store, a second unit was opened and, step by step, the independent owner increased his business through careful management and sound business methods.

The capital for the added stores came from within the organization itself. When we look at the success of the large chain store of today, we must remember that in nearly every case the expansion came from within and that the financing was not based upon floating stock. Here lies the secret of the great financial strength of many of our present chain organizations.

During the period of development, from 1900 to 1918, we witnessed startling industrial and social changes which made fertile soil for the increased success of the chain store. During these years the automobile came into general use, thus bringing the people of the farm, country, and small towns to the larger cities. More and more, people began to do their trading in the larger centers of population. Then came the World War with its demands for mass production and standardized goods. Naturally, the tendency towards mass production played directly into the hands of the chain store with its fundamental principle of mass distribution. Along with all these changes, came the psychology for doing things in a big

way. People began to think in terms of millions and billions
instead of thousands and hundreds of thousands.

THE GREAT PROGRESS OF CHAINS IN A DECADE--Since the war,
that is since 1919.....the chain store industry has expanded
with a rapidity that made even its previous expansion seem
relatively slow. The post-war boom was a tonic to the chain
...everywhere new chains were established and old chains
enlarged.

Authoritative figures revealing for comparison the size
and sales volume of the chain store industry in the year following the ending of the World War are not available. Reliable estimates, however, establish the volume of chain store
business in America, in that year, at approximately four per
cent of the total retail trade of the country.

Within three years...that is, by 1923...chain store
business mounted to six per cent; by 1926 to eight per cent;
by 1927 to twelve per cent...and by the end of 1929, to twenty
per cent of our nation's total retail business.

By 1933, according to the United States Census of American
Business for that year, the chain store's share of the nation's
total retail trade had increased to 25.2%. In other words,
in the space of thirteen years--from 1920 to 1933--the chain
store industry increased its share of the retail trade in
this country by more than six times.

18

PERIOD FOLLOWING THE WORLD WAR--The period of expansion
or rapid growth, which followed the World War, is from our
point of view the most remarkable period of all, for it was
in these years that we actually witnessed the phenomenal
growth of the chain store. We saw a wave of expansion, both
in the number of stores and in the volume of business, which
exceeded the fondest hopes of the most optimistic chain store
executives. Never before had this country witnessed such a
revolution in retail distribution. In less than ten years the
total volume of business among chains was more than quad-
rupled. It is estimated that in 1921, chain store business
of all kinds accounted for only four per cent of the total
retail trade in the United States. According to Dr. Paul H.
Nystrom of Columbia University, chain stores did six per cent
of the retail business in 1923, eight per cent in 1927,
twelve per cent in 1928 and eighteen per cent in 1929. The
total number of chain systems, counting all concerns with
two or more units, will probably amount to eight thousand
operating according to the most recent estimate of the National
Chain Store Association, 168,000 stores. Estimates of the
total volume of business done by the chain stores amounts to
approximately more than nine billion dollars. The United
States Bureau of Census for 1930, reports that the total volume of business done by retail units amounts to the staggering
sum of fifty billion, thirty-three million dollars. The 1930

census figures show that there are one million, five hundred
and forty-nine thousand retail stores in the forty-eight
states and the District of Columbia, or 12.6 stores per one
thousand inhabitants and that the average store does an annual business of $32,297 and the average per capita pur-
chases at retail amount to $497.52. Using the estimates of
most authorities that chains do from eighteen to twenty per
cent of the retail business, we may safely conclude that
chains do approximately nine and a half billion dollars worth
of business annually.

PRESENT PERIOD OF CHAIN STORE GROWTH--At the present
time chains have gained their greatest prominence in the
grocery field, where, according to the United States Bureau
of Census for 1930, they are operating from fifty-five thousand to fifty-seven thousand stores and are doing approximately forty per cent of the volume of business. Also, much
progress has recently been made in the drug field, where
chains operate approximately four thousand stores, doing more
than twenty per cent of the business. In the five and ten
cent field, chains command more than fifty per cent of the
retail trade. In fact, chains today have entered almost every
known branch of mercantile distribution and while their growth
at present has been generally retarded, their limit of expansion has not been reached. Such prominent authorities as
Dr. Paul H. Nystrom of Columbia University, Professor James

20

L. Palmer of Chicago University and others believe that
chains will continue to expand slowly in most fields of
retailing for some time to come. [1]

CHAIN STORE GROWTH EXPLAINED--Unqualified, these figures indicating the tremendous growth of the chain store industry from 1920 through 1933 may serve chain store enemies
usefully in supporting their charges that chain stores are
rapidly moving to a point where they will ultimately monop-
olize the retail trade of the United States.

If these figures are given thoughtful consideration,
however, it will soon become evident that the chain stores,
in expanding their business from four per cent of the total
retail trade in the country in 1919, to twenty per cent of
the aggregate retail business in America in 1929, were not
alone in achieving noteworthy business progress. Further
study of the subject will reveal that chain stores were...
during this decade...merely in the swim of a business cycle
that was rapidly moving to the peak of American prosperity...
a peak that was finally reached in 1929.

The fact that the chain store share of the total retail
trade of this country jumped, during the depression period
from 1929 to 1933, from twenty per cent in 1929 to 24.2% in
1933 is explained by the United States Bureau of the Census
on the following page. [2]

[1] Buehler pp. 7-13
[2] (Reference source: Census of American Business, Retail
Volume 1, pp. 25 and 26.)

21

"The higher chain ratio in 1933 for retail trade as a
whole does not mean that the chains in all kinds of business
have weathered the four years of depression better than independents. Much of the cause of the smaller aggregate decline
in the chain stores than in the independent sales is the relatively smaller decline in the sales of those kinds of business
in which the chains prefer to operate,--food, variety and drug
stores, and filling stations. In these four fields, which account for more than one-half of total chain store sales, the
decline in sales between 1929 and 1933 (for chains and independent combined) average thirty-four per cent, compared with
fifty-six per cent in all the other business fields together.
In most of those kinds of business which experienced the greatest decline in sales volume, chains are a negligible factor."

DECLINING PRICES AND ECONOMY--Let us turn for a moment
to a study of the basic economic conditions of the country
from 1921 to the present. The Smithsonian Institution--seeing
prices crumble after 1919--determined to find out from a study
of business movements, after other great wars, what was ahead
for our business interests. From the data that were assembled
it was found that, after both the Napoleanic and the Civil War,
prices and business experienced a sudden depression that wiped
out roughly fifty per cent of the war time inflation, after
which the period of falling prices was slowly spread out over
a span of twenty years.

22

THE LONG-TIME MOVEMENT OF PRICES AND THE CHAIN STORE

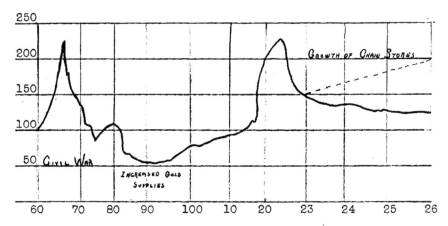

This, in a broad way, is what we have experienced since
the World War. From the deflation and general unemployment
of 1920 and 1921, there emerged an entirely new class of con-
sumers--a class forced to save by dire necessity. Whereas,
during the era of rising prices and accelerated war-time growth
from 1895 to 1920, the great middle class insisted on service,
they were glad to forego this for price from 1921 on.

Those who had in the past locked with disdain on chain
stores in general found themselves welcoming them with open
arms. With the reduction of the consumer's dollar to fifty-
six cents from 1914--1920, with a number of items, such as
rent, insurance, etc., remaining as fixed overhead, the house-
wife turned first to food economy through the medium of the
multiple store, with its cash-and-carry appeal.

23

RELATIVE GROWTH IN VARIOUS FIELDS--The necessity for
economy, while it stimulated the multiple store with its
many buying, managing and merchandising advantages, bene-
fited those fields most, in which tne individual purchase
is small and in which, service is not the determining factor.
Grocery, five and ten, candy, drug and cigar chains, show the
most rapid growth. The chain store is now represented in a-
bout fifty-five different fields in this country. Where it
takes but three thousand dollars for each store and ordinary
business management to open new outlets in the grocery field,
an entirely different situation prevails in the drug field.
To open a chain drug store takes at least twenty thousand dollars in net capital to equip and stock with merchandise.

AMERICAN CHAINS ABROAD--While the leading American chains
would seem to have plenty to do keeping pace with this domes-
tic expansion programs, they have not neglected the possibil-
ities of foreign markets. Expansion in other countries is by
no means visionary--it has passed the discussion point and is
already a basic reality. Germany is the country usually selected, for the following reasons:

(1) It has a number of first and second class cities
which lend themselves most readily to new retail outlets.

(2) Germany has the largest population on the Continent
(excluding Russia).

(3) Consumers are thrifty and progressive.

24

The F. W. Woolworth Company has for some time operated
a profitable English subsidiary and has recently begun to
enter Germany on a large scale, locating the first stores at
Bremen, Berlin, Dusseldorf, and Wiesbaden. The firm also has
had a satisfactory return from its six Cuban outlets. The
English subsidiary did from twenty-five to thirty per cent
more business during 1927, than during 1926, and brought its
total number of outlets to 290, with the addition of fifty
stores during 1927. A five and ten cent organization spon-
sored by Leonard Feitz has been successful, while the chain-
store system of "Hadepe", in the same country, selling at
the fifty pfenning price range failed.

All who have studied the field are agreed that Canada
presents unusual opportunities to American chains for expansion. Mr. Baxter believes grocery chain sales alone will
exceed fifty million dollars in Ontario and Quebec, with those
of buying groups estimated at forty-three million dollars.
In Toronto already over twenty per cent of the grocery business is done by chains and buying groups. Approximately one-
third of the business done will be handled by two organization
The Dominion Stores and Lovelaw's Groceteria. The Atlantic
and Pacific Tea Company has opened fifty stores and has an
extensive program planned. The Fanny Farmer candy stores
changed their name to Laura Secord across the border. Even
our well-known Child's restaurants have outlets in Winnipeg
and Ottawa.

IN OTHER COUNTRIES--In Japan there is a chain of drug
stores with two thousand units and five thousand more plan-
ned--the Hoshi Pharmaceutical Company. The bulk of merchandise sold is comprised of the Company's private brands, although of late other brands are being taken on. Even in
Egypt fifty per cent of the country's entire drug volume is
in the hands of a single chain known as Societe Anonyme des
Dregneries d'Egypte. This chain has thirty-six stores and
wholesale houses and four warehouses.

England has been quick to utilize the advantages presented by chain store merchandising on a large scale commercial basis. Boots the Chemists, operated by United Drug
Company of this country comprises a system of over eight
hundred units. The organization has been operating for over
fifty-one years, gradually evolving from the original herb
shops owned by Boots to the present enormous drug chain system. Although the Boots organization is owned by the same
interests as the Louis K. Liggett Company in America, the two
companies operate on radically different policies. The small-
est independent druggist in England sells most of its leading
articles just as cheaply as the largest drug chain. Price
maintenance is within the law in England and manufacturers are
permitted to control the resale price of their products. Nine
per cent of the drug stores of Great Britain belong to the
Proprietary Articles Trade Association in cooperation with
manufacturers and jobbers, all of whom are agreed on a fixed

price policy. Although Boots manufacture approximately three
per cent of their products on which they set their own prices,
all remaining products are price-fixed. Hence, it is apparent
that Boots rely mainly on superior service and clever merchandising. Boots are adding new stores at the rate of fifty per
year and have one unit to every fifty thousand people and to
every one hundred and twenty square miles of England. This
chain alone represents the high standard of British initiative
in the drug chain field.

ALL LINES REPRESENTED--The Liggett drug interests control the five hundred Boots drug outlets in Great Britain,
and the Schulte firm, besides running the Dunhill shops in
England, operates stores in Paris and Monte Carlo. In the
shoe field the Walkover shoe Company numbers about fifty outlets in practically every capital city of the world. The
magnitude of the expansion program of American chains abroad
may be gleaned from the negotiations carried on this year between the United Cigar interests and the French government
for the tobacco monopoly of that country.

In the restaurant chain field the House of Lyons is outstanding. This unusual organization operates over two hundred
tea shops, restaurants, and confectionery stores in London and
throughout the British provinces. The service of Lyon's ("nip-
pies", girl waitresses) is a byword in England and might well
be studied by restaurant chain systems in America. The "ABC"
restaurants and tea shops also operate an extensive chain syste

IV

POLICIES OF CHAIN STORES

27

FUNDAMENTAL FACTORS IN CHAIN STORE OPERATION--The mere
fact that the three leading chain grocery systems alone did
slightly under one billion five hundred thousand dollars in
business during 1930, with net earnings of forty million dollars, testifies to the soundness of chain stores. There are
certain fundamental features common to chains in all lines.
In the first place, the chain reaches its greatest success in
those fields in which consumers most frequently purchase standardized articles. For instnace there were two hundred and
seventy-four million pairs of all-silk hose sold in this country last year, the average girl in the large cities buying a
pair every three weeks. Naturally, such a commodity, that
sells itself and requires little service, is ideal for chain-
store operation. On the other hand, in an optical store,
where each client must be treated differently by high-priced
men, and where the consumer buys but once a year, the forces
are somewhat in favor of the individual operator. The basic
principles of chain store operation are:

1. The exterior and interior of the store must "appeal
to the eye",--especially if the article sold deals with women.
(Child's, Fanny Farmer).

2. The commodity sold must require little or no personal
service.

3. It should be an article that the consumer purchases
quite often during the year, permitting large turnover at low
profits. (Tobacco, groceries, candy, fruit).

4. Articles that are standardized, requiring little

28

5. The average sale must not be large or the merchandise so bulky that deliveries are made necessary.

6. The territory served should be one in which the units are not too far apart to permit of supervision and supply from centrally located warehouses.

The following statistics show the amount spent by each resident of Baltimore in a year, thus giving one an idea of the fields in which the chain may be most successful:

Groceries	$68.17	Drugs	$13.93
Furniture	20.89	Men's Wear	13.53
Hardware	10.71	Candy	8.31
Shoes	7.52	Women's Wear	9.44
Jewelry	6.72	Auto Accessories	5.38
Tobacco	4.53	Radio	1.21

Department Stores $104.21

Small Investment Per Store---When Herbert Hoover assumed charge of the department of Commerce, one of his first steps was to emphasize the necessity for standardized products in industry, with the elimination of too many styles and too many models in various lines. The Chain store has followed this suggestion with unusually good results.

29

Capital Per Store (1926)

F. W. Woolworth	$43,918	Walgreen Company	$33,000
American Stores	4,300	Waldorf System	55,000
Kroger Company	5,000	Child's Restaurant	185,000
Atlantic and Pacific	4,300	J. C. Penney	25,332
Fanny Farmer ·	12,500	United Cigar	20,000
Melville Shoe	20,000	Richman Brothers	170,000

To eculp a candy store similar to the Fanny Farmer type it takes but $3,000 in additional capital, whereas for a new chain drug store it requires $20,000. Naturally, the more capital per store necessary the slower the rate of expansion.

Almost every grocery system is constantly besieged by manufacturers of all types of novelties to take on their line, but in most cases, unless some unusual inducements are present, the system will not add it to its list of items carried, which, for the most successful companies, varies from nine hundred and fifty to one thousand and twenty-five items. As it is, the order sheet of the store manager covers the top of an ordinary-sized desk.

Probably the greatest number of items carried is in the case of the chain drug stores with approximately eight thousand items. In the shoe field, stores of the Thom McAnn type are the most profitable, there being a number of cases of these stores having a complete turnover in one day on the Saturday preceding Easter.

30

Margin of Profit on Sales

F. W. Woolworth-------11.12%	J. C. Penney---------7.15%
Melville Shoe----------6.65%	Frank B. Shattuck---10.38%
Waldorf System---------9.95%	The Great A. & P.
Child's---------------10.84%	Tea Company-----2.90%
Average Ten New York	American Stores------6.3%
Chain Grocers----1.50%	Piggly Wiggly
Kroger----------------4.10%	Western--------2.1%

One of the basic principles of chain store success is the necessity for rapid turnover. The best example of this is fresh vegetables, which have a turnover of three a week. A large system can have in its inventory several millions in vegetables without having any of its capital tied up. The merchandise need not be paid for, for ten days, and the money is realized two days after it is received, thereby permitting the chain to have the use of this money for a week or so for nothing.

The American Stores of Philadelphia alone have built up a fund of over two million dollars by taking two per cent discounts on the bulk of their purchases. Several instances have arisen where an individual would start a small chain of twenty-five stores in a rural district with practically no capital, paying for his merchandise in thirty days, after he had sold it himself.

Some chains carry for more cash than they can use in their business. For example, the Richman Brothers clothing

chain of Cleveland had one hundred thousand dollars in cash
or Liberty Bonds for each store. A number of chains practically finance themselves on manufacturer's money. One chain
of sporting-goods and radio stores usually gets a sixty to
ninety day credit on its major supplies and sells the merchandise within a month, thus having the free use of the money for
the remaining period.

The most desirable items undoubtedly are those with a
daily or weekly turnover, such as bread, vegetables, and meat.
Here the chain gets a ten day credit and at no time does it
have any of its own money involved, the money being in the bank
drawing interest for several days before due.

A Major or Minor Produce?--In determining the probable
success for a new chain or the extent to which an old one may
progress, one must give considerable attention to the possibility of the merchandise sold being taken up by a chain in a different field. For example, every chain drug store in the country is specializing more each year on the food business, thus
making it evident that "sandwich shops" and straight restaurant
chains will ultimately feel the competition. A few examples of
this trend are:

1. The grocery chains are entering the cigarette and
tobacco business and also offering serious competition to
bakery chains.

2. The cigar chains are featuring candy and minor drug
lines.

3. The men's hat chains are adding top-coats, ties,

32

4. The men's clothing chains are going into women's sport lines.

5. The grocery chains are turning decidedly to meat, house-hold utensils, drug lines, candy, dry pack ice cream, soft drinks, and hardware.

6. The drug chains in some cases are adding books and department store items and radios.

7. Five-and-ten cent stores now have food products, restaurants, and articles of apparel such as hosiery and underwear.

8. Department stores often carry one hundred and fifty drug items, are considering luncheonettes and in one California City have cut groceries so low that the business is no longer profitable for anyone.

9. Such organizations as Montgomery-Ward are opening special tire outlets.

10. Shoe stores are adding hosiery and other knit goods.

CHAIN STORES AND PUBLIC POLICY--There has been no new economic movement in this country which in its early inception was not bitterly fought. Unfortunately, the chain grocery stores are bearing the brunt of such attacks today, especially in the Western states. Of course, in time, not only business interests, but the public, as well, will recognize the immense service that the chain form of distribution has performed in bringing American business to its present height of prosperity.

33

One can study carefully the policies of the Great Atlantic and Pacific Tea Company, the Woolworth Company, and the J. C. Penney Company in dealing with manufacturers, independent competitors, and the public, and find that they have pursued policies that have been a credit to these organizations since their start. After studying the life of the independent merchant under the old system of distribution and comparing it with that of a manager of a chain store, it is evident that the present chain system is far superior.

"Service Features in Chain Stores"--Letter from the Chairman of the Federal Trade Commission.

Sec. 1. Under Senate Resolution 224, the Federal Trade Commission was directed to inquire into and report to the Senate regarding--The advantages or disadvantages of chain store distribution in comparison with those of other types of distribution as shown by prices, costs, profits, and margins, quality of goods and services rendered by chain stores and other distributors or resulting from integration, managerial efficiency, low overhead, or other similar causes. This report on the service features in chain stores is primarily based on detailed information obtained from returns to the original chain-store schedule. Additional information was obtained by field agents from chain-store executives. It is intended to show the relative extent and importance of service features, such as the extension of credit, the giving

of free delivery service, and the taking of telephone orders
in various kinds of chains.

Sec. 2. Extent of the use of a cash or credit policy.
All chains reporting--This section presents a detailed break-
down of the proportions of chains, their stores and net sales,
operating on the following bases: (a) Cash--all stores of the
chain selling strictly for cash, or where credit sales as a
whole are negligible (1% of sales, or less), (b) Full credit--
all stores of the chain allowing or extending credit to all
customers who are considered good credit risks, (c) limited
credit--all stores of the chain extending credit to some customers, and (d) combination--stores of a chain not operating
on any uniform policy but using two or all three of the above-
mentioned bases. Some stores of a particular chain may sell
strictly for cash, some may extend credit to all good credit
risks, while still other stores may only extend credit to some
customers.

In using the terms "full credit," "limited credit," and
"combination," no implication is intended that such stores do
not sell also for cash. The analyses of this report are intended to ascertain the relative importance of the business
done on a credit basis in addition to sales made for cash.

The following table shows the proportion of chains operating on the different bases of credit policy in 1928, together with the number of stores operated and the volume of
business transacted. Table on page 35.

35

DISTRIBUTION OF CHAINS, STORES, AND SALES ACCORDING TO CREDIT
POLICY, 1928

Credit Policy	Chains		Stores		Sales	
	Number	%	Number	%	Amount	%
All Stores:						
Cash [1]	909	53.5	57,785	87.5	$3,744,787,902	72.9
Full Credit [2]	557	32.8	4,007	6.1	1,069,136,574	20.8
Limited Credit[3]	45	2.6	578	.9	87,746,579	1.7
Combination[4]	189	11.1	3,614	5.5	238,170,822	4.6
Total	1,700	100.0	65,984	100.0	5,139,841,877	100.0

DIFFERENT KINDS OF CHAINS--A majority of chains in sixteen of the twenty-six kinds of business report all stores on
a cash basis, while in only seven lines of business did one-
half or more of the chains report all stores extending credit
to all customers who were good credit risks. The remaining
three kinds of chains, men's ready-to-wear, dry goods and apparel, and women's ready-to-wear, show no decided concentration of chains in any one of the specified credit bases.

[1] Chains reporting a negligible amount of credit (1% or less
of total sales) have been included as operating all stores
on a cash basis.

[2] Extended credit in all stores to all customers who were
proper credit risks.

[3] Extended credit in all stores to some customers.

[4] Operated some stores on any two or all three of the above
bases.

36

All unlimited-price variety and nearly all dollar-limit
variety, and the hat and cap chains operated all their units
on a strictly cash basis. In addition, eighty to eighty-six
per cent of the chains in the five-dollar-limit variety, confectionery, men's shoes, women's accessories, and men's furnishings reported all stores on a cash basis. Approximately
three-fourths of the grocery chains and about two-thirds of
the men's and women's shoes, tobacco, dry goods, and the
grocery and meat chains sold for cash.

On the other hand, all chains reporting in the musical
instruments and furniture group extended credit in all stores
to all good credit risks while about eighty per cent of the
chains in the hardware and general merchandise fields, seventy-
five per cent of the men's and women's ready-to-wear and depart
ment store chains, and one half of the chains in the drug group
reported all stores on a full credit basis. Of the twenty-six
kinds of business, fifteen disclose one or more chains with
all units extending credit to only some customers. The number
of chains in any group which reported operating on this basis
is less than ten per cent. Six groups show but one chain on
a limited credit basis. Chains which do not operate all stores
on the same credit basis are found in twenty out of the twenty-
six types of business studied. The largest proportion of
chains on this combination basis is that of the millinery
group with approximately forty per cent, followed by dry goods

and apparel and women's ready-to-wear with nearly twenty per
cent. The remaining groups show ratios of less than thirteen
per cent.

In seventeen of the twenty-six kinds of business the
proportion of chains operating all stores on a cash basis to
the total answering the questions on credit policy is smaller
than is the proportion of stores operated by these chains.
Conversely, the proportion of chains extending credit in all
stores to all customers who are good credit risks is materially
larger in fifteen of these seventeen kinds of business than is
the proportion of stores operated, the exception being dollar-
limit variety and men's and women's ready-to-wear. Two additional groups, women's shoes and department store, show percentage of chains on a full credit basis which is considerably
larger than is the percentage of stores operated.

In the grocery and meat group, for example, 64.8% of the
reporting chains sold for cash in 1928, yet these same chains
operated 96.1% of the stores operated by all reporting chains
in the group, while the twenty-one per cent of the chains extending credit to all good credit risks operated only one per
cent of the total stores. Two thirds of the tobacco group
chain-store organizations were on a cash basis, but these
chains operated nearly all (97.2%) of the stores reported by
the chains of the tobacco group. The 15.1% of tobacco chains
on a full credit basis, however, accounted for only 1.1% of

the stores. In the dry goods and apparel trade, less than
one half (46.8%) of the chain sold primarily for cash, yet
accounted for 81.9% of the stores operated but 6.9% of the
total stores. Slightly less than one third (32%) of the drug
chains were on a cash basis and operated approximately two
thirds (65.7%) of the stores reported for the drug group,
while one half of the chains in this kind of business were on
a full credit basis but operated only one sixth (16.5%) of the
total stores.

On the other hand, six kinds of business (men's furnishings, women's accessories, millinery, women's shoes, department store, and hardware) show a larger percentage of chains
operating all stores on a cash basis than they show of stores
operated, while five kinds of chains, including four of the
above, disclose a smaller percentage of chains on a full credit
basis than they show of stores operated. In none of these instances are the differences outstanding.

Of the fifteen kinds of business which reported one or
more chains operating all stores on a limited credit basis,
three show a larger percentage of stores than they do of
chains, while the opposite is true of twelve kinds of business. In the department store group, one chain reported a
limited use of credit in all stores, yet this concern operated
37.7% of the stores operated by all reporting chains in this
group.

39

In five of the twenty kinds of business revealing one
or more chains operating some stores, on any two or all three
of the specified credit basis (cash, full credit, and limited
credit), the proportion of chains thus operating to the total
reporting is smaller than is the proportion of stores operated.
For example, less than ten per cent of the reporting women's
shoe chains followed this practice, yet these same chains
accounted for nearly one third (31.2% of the total stores of
this group. On the other hand, fourteen lines of business
show a larger percentage of chains on a combination basis
than they show of stores operated. In the dry goods and apparel group, approximately one fifth of the chains did not
follow a uniform policy in all stores in respect to credit,
but operated only one tenth of the total stores reported in
this group. The grocery group alone showed the same proportion of chains on this basis as of stores operated.

There is a prevailing tendency in the larger chains to
operate all stores on a cash basis or to extend credit in
some stores only. Chains on any other basis are, in general,
materially below average size.

Sec. 3. Extent of credit and cash business of six hundred and thirty-one chains granting credit.--

The schedule requested chains that did not sell strictly
for cash to report the proportion of their total sales transacted on a credit basis. All chains reporting a negligible
amount of credit business or stating it to be 1% or less of

their total net sales were considered as chains selling for
cash.

Furniture chains granting at least some credit revealed
the greatest extension of this service, 85.2% of their total
sales being on a credit basis. Musical instrument chains
ranked second with 74.5% of the total sales for credit, followed by the men's and women's ready-to-wear group with 69.2%
of their sales on this basis. Other kinds of chains ranked
in descending order according to the relative importance of
their extension of credit were as follows: Hardware (54.4%),
General Merchandise (47.6%), Women's ready-to-wear (44.7%),
Women's Shoes (39.2%), Men's ready-to-wear (38.9%), Department
Store (35.9%), and Millinery(31.7%). Returns from ten other
kinds of chains, including the three food groups, men's and
women's shoes, and dry goods and apparel, indicate that between 16.4% and 27.4% of the total sales of chains extending
credit to customers were transacted on a credit basis in 1928.
The drug group, with the largest number of reporting credit
chains, however, reported less than ten per cent of the total
sales as made on a credit basis. In only three kinds of
chains--men's and women's ready-to-wear, furniture, and musical instruments--did any chains report all their sales as
being on a credit basis. In these same kinds of business,
substantial proportions of the total credit chains reported
eighty to ninety-nine per cent of their goods sold on credit.
In general merchandise almost one half of the chains reported

from sixty to seventy-nine per cent, while in the department-
store field over one half of the chains stated that forty to
fifty-nine per cent of their sales were on a credit basis.

The grocery, meat, drug, millinery, men's and women's
shoes, and dry goods and apparel groups show a great majority
of the chains,(two-thirds or more) with less than forty per
cent of their goods sold on credit. Furthermore, in the grocery and drug fields over one half of the credit chains reported that the business transacted on a credit basis was
less than twenty per cent.

Sec. 4. Policies of chains granting occasional credit--

In the case of grocery chains, the Cloverdale Company,
operating two hundred and sixty-eight stores on December 31,
1928, estimated that in sixty of these stores credit was extended to hospitals, churches, town officers, and restaurants.
Daniel Reeves, Inc., stated: "We do substantially a cash
business, any debts would be exceptional. Credit would be
given only in exceptional cases merely as an accommodation."[1]

Several of the larger grocery and meat chains extended a
negligible amount of credit. The Great Atlantic and Pacific
Tea Company asserts that: This company sells strictly for
cash at all of its stores. Occasionally we find that some
store managers extend credit to a selected few of their customers; they do so on their own responsibility, and it is a
personal matter between them and their customers, for which

[1] Report of Federal Trade Commission--1936

they are personally liable, as it is not in accord with the
company's policy. Such sales, however, are trivial, amounting to a small fraction of one per cent.

This company further states--No credit is extended, business being done on a strictly cash-and-carry basis. Some ex-
perimenting has been done, however, with credit and deliveries, in territories where competitive conditions and the trading habits of customers seem to demand it, but neither delivery
nor credit has become the established policy or practice of
the company at large.

The Kroger Grocery and Baking Company states that all
sales are cash except institutional, charity and school accounts. In a statement to a field agent of the Commission
this company asserts that "We do not extend credit to any
customers and it is strictly against the policy of the company to do so," [1] but goes on to give an example of a manager who did and was transferred on account of the company's
policy. The Red Owl Stores, Inc. states that some stores extend credit to institutional accounts authorized by central
office.

In a statement to a Commission's field agent the H. C.
Bohack Company asserts that:

The company tries to operate on a strictly cash basis
and has a rule that any credit accounts must be authorized
by headquarters. The company was founded on a cash basis

[1] Report of Federal Trade Commission--1936

and ninety-nine per cent of the business is on a cash basis.
We get requests frequently from some individual whose husband
holds such-and-such a position in a New York bank, and she
wants credit. We reply generally with a form letter declining
to give it. Some few exceptions are made in cases of big es-
tates on Long Island.

Of the drug chains, the Dow Drug Company reports: Our
credit business is very small, merely occasional accommodation,
though we do it regularly, and the Louis K. Ligget Company
states that: The policy of the business is to sell only for
cash. In rare cases only is an exception made, where credit
might be extended temporarily by the store manager to a known
customer, or temporarily in continuation of a policy of a
predecessor store.

Among the confectionery chains, Huyler's states that all
stores extend credit to some customers but that this credit
business does not exceed one per cent of their total sales.
In this same group, the Nunnally Company extends credit in
all stores but reports it to be only one half of one per cent
of its total business.

The S. H. Kress Company reports that some stores extended thirty-day credits to a limited number of public institutions such as hospitals, colleges, army posts, etc.,
as an accommodation, but that the proportion of credit sales
is negligible. The W. T. Grant Company made the following

statement to a field agent of the Commission regarding credit:

None, whatever, however, our company has a separate organization selling wearing apparel, chiefly on the second
floor of certain stores. We have had difficulty in getting
tenants for some of our upstairs spaces so we took over a
ready-to-wear organization that occupied such space in certain
of our stores, and we are now operating twelve wearing apparel
stores in our upstairs space. These stores permit a customer
to buy coats or dresses on the "lay-by" plan, under which the
garment is set aside for them while they pay installments of
the total price.

Among the wearing apparel chains the Martins Store Corporation reports that one of its seven stores, extends credit
to some customers but that they took over this store which did
some credit business, and are now converting it slowly into
strictly all cash. The Lunstrom Hat Works, Inc. reported
their credit business to be less than one tenth of one per
cent, "merely accommodation to friends of the executives."[1]
The Graham Department Stores extended credit only to hospitals, churches, charitable institutions, etc.

The Florsheim Shoe Store Company stated that all its
stores extended credit to some customers but that the total
credit business was only one per cent of their total retail
sales. A few stores of Sheppard-Meyers, Inc., gave credit
accommodation to charitable institutions. The I. H. Morse

[1] Report of Federal Trade Commission--1936

45

Shoe Stores operating eight units extended credit in three,
two of which were department stores which assumed the risk,
and these credit sales were estimated at one per cent.

The J. C. Penney Company, made the following statement
to a Commission's field agent:

No credit is given. Merchandise may be selected and put
aside on a small payment to be delivered on final payment of
purchase. The length of time an article may be held depends
entirely upon the community. It may be held from ten days to
a month, but this is a practice that is discouraged.

Sec. 8. Extent of free-delivery service to customers.
Classification of delivery service--the following policies
are employed by chain stores with regard to deliveries: (a)
No delivery service, (b) Full delivery service, (c) Limited
delivery service, (d) Combination delivery service.

The first grant is composed of those chains which report that none of their stores make any deliveries whatsoever or which report that the amount of goods delivered free
of charge to customers is negligible. The full delivery service group includes all chains reporting that all stores offer
full delivery service free of charge to all customers; the
limited service group, those chains reporting that all
stores make some delivery to some customers free of charge;
while the combination group includes those chains which report some stores giving no delivery service, and some stores
giving limited delivery service, or any two of these three.

Delivery Policy	Chains		Stores		Sales	
	Number	%	Number	%	Amount	%
All Stores:						
No delivery[1]	927	54.9	53,199	80.8	$3,555,775,881	69.2
Full delivery[2]	513	30.4	6,515	9.9	1,163,946,704	22.7
Limited delivery[3]	132	7.8	1,956	3.0	216,272,695	4.2
Combination[4]	117	6.9	4,178	6.3	199,802,821	3.9
Total	1,689	100.0	65,848	100.0	5,135,789,191	100.0

Delivery policies of all reporting chains.--Of the one tho
sand six hundred and eighty-nine chains reporting for the year
1928, over one half (54.9%) either stated that no stores made
deliveries to customers or reported such deliveries to be of
negligible proportions; while slightly over thirty per cent of
these chains reported all stores giving full delivery service.
The 54.9 per cent of the chain-store organizations that reported all stores on a non-delivery basis accounted for four
fifths (80.8%) of the total sales of the one thousand six
hundred eighty-nine chain store systems. Chains on a full

[1] Negligible amount (254 chains considered as not making deliveries.)
[2] Full delivery service.
[3] Some deliveries free of charge
[4] Operated some stores on any two or three of the abov-mentioned bases.

delivery basis, while operating only 9.9% of the stores of
all reporting chains in 1928, accounted for 22.7% of the total net sales. A total of one hundred and thirty two chains
or merely eight per cent of the total, reported that all stores
made some deliveries to customers free of charge. This group
operated but three per cent of the total stores and accounted
for about four per cent of the total volume of business.
Slightly under seven per cent of the reporting chains do not
follow the same practice in all their stores, but may use some
conbination of full delivery, no delivery, or limited delivery,
in part of their stores. This latter group of chains account
for about six and four per cent respectively, of the total
stores and net sales of all chains combined.

Sec. 13. Extent of the practice of taking telephone
orders from customers.

Reports are received from one thousand and forty-nine
chains giving the number of stores which took telephone orders
from customers, either to be delivered to the customer's home
or to be called for later at the store.

The table on the following page shows the number and
proportion of chains that reported on the practice of taking
telephone orders from customers in 1928, together with the
number and proportion of stores operated and the total net
sales.

DISTRIBUTION OF CHAINS, STORES, AND SALES ACCORDING TO
EXTENT OF PRACTICE OF TAKING TELEPHONE ORDERS IN 1928.

Telephone Orders taken by------	Chains		Stores		Sales	
	Number	%	Number	%	Amount	%
No Stores	768	51.2	31,386	49.4	$2,340,497,062	47.3
All Stores	620	41.4	7,696	12.1	1,260,669,708	25.4
Some Stores	111	7.4	24,499	38.5	1,353,215,644	27.3
Total	1,499	100.0	63,581	100.0	4,954,382,414	100.0

A little over one half (51.2%) of the reporting chains
stated that none of their stores accepted telephone orders
in 1928. These chains account for slightly less than one half
of the stores (49,4%) and sales (47.3%) reported by the one
thousand and four hundred and ninety-nine chains. A somewhat
smaller number, or 41.4% of all the chains reporting for that
year, stated that all stores took telephone orders from customers. These chains, while operating only 12.1% of the total
stores of all reporting chains in 1928, accounted for twenty-
five and four tenths per cent of the total net sales. A total of one hundred and eleven chains, or seven per cent of all
reporting chains, took telephone orders in some of their stores
This group operated nearly forty per cent of the total stores
and accounted for about 2.7% of the total volume of business.
The data in the above table would appear to indicate that the
policy of taking telephone orders in all store is more general
among the smaller chains than the larger.

49

Sec. 16.--Extent of a cash-and-carry policy.--Seven hundred and twenty-three chains, or nearly eighty per cent of all reporting cash chains, gave no free delivery service. The seven hundred and twenty-three cash-and-carry chains accounted for about ninety per cent of all stores and sales reported by chains on a cash basis. All the general merchandise chains on a cash basis reported no free deliveries. Following in order of the proportions of chains which sold for cash and did not deliver, are dollar-limit variety (93.9%), women's accessories (92.3%), tobacco (90.9%), men's furnishings (89.3%), and men's and women's shoes (86.6%).

In nine groups (general merchandise, tobacco, grocery, and meat, dry goods and apparel, women's accessories, dollar-limit variety, men's furnishings, men's and women's shoes, and five-dollar-limit variety) over twelve per cent of the stores belonging to all chains selling for cash were operated by chains which also gave practically no free-delivery service.

A comparison of the proportion of chains with those of the stores operated by them discloses that in sixteen of the twenty-three lines of business the proportions of chains are smaller than the proportions of stores operated, while in six cases the opposite is true. In the general merchandise group, all chains selling for cash made no deliveries whatsoever.

Sec. 17. Delivery at customer's expense.--Seventy-six chains operating nine thousand, eight hundred and twenty-seven stores reported that they made deliveries at customer's

expense. These deliveries were made in a variety of ways, such as by own delivery equipment, outside delivery systems, boys at store, messengers, parcel post, and express. The great majority of these sixteen chains offered no free-delivery service although a few companies delivered free of charge when purchases exceeded a certain amount and made a charge for delivery of purchases under this amount.

Slightly over one half of the chains reporting deliveries at customer's expense are in the grocery and grocery-and-meat fields, and one of their chains accounts for over one half of the total stores reported. The remainder of the chains are scattered over sixteen lines of business and range from five companies in the men's and women's shoe field down to one chain in each of six lines. Stores and sales vary widely between the sixteen kinds of business.

In the grocery and grocery-and-meat lines it seems to be the practice for the deliveries of chains making a charge for this service to be made either by store clerks in their spare moments, or by boys, or by outside delivery companies.

The National Tea Company reports that deliveries are made to customers "through independent neighborhood delivery service" and that the "customer makes arrangements for delivery and pays the cost of same to person making delivery.

Sear, Roebuck and Company reported that--In Sears,Roebuck and Company's stores the cash-and-carry policy prevails

except on such lines of merchandise that are large and heavy
and of such a nature that they cannot easily be carried out
by the customer, in which cases the retail-store manager adds
to the selling price, drayage charges figured on local rates.

V

ADVANTAGES OF CHAIN STORES

52

CHAIN STORE ADVANTAGES: The business advantages of chain stores are those points of commercial superiority which are not commonly enjoyed by the rank and file of their competitors. Though there are many of them, by far the most important are the buying advantages and the relatively low cost of doing business which the chains have effectuated.

BUYING ADVANTAGES: That the chain store has had a decided advantage over the independent in the matter of buying is quite freely admitted. Chains purchase in vast quantities, take advantage of cash discounts, and place their orders at opportune times. The net result is that they secure the very lowest prices which the markets afford. This ability to purchase advantageously extends beyond the merchandise bout for resale; it includes supplies, store fixtures, advertising, equipment, and other materials. Probably no single factor has been of greater importance in the success of chain store merchandising than the buying advantage.

QUANTITY PURCHASING.--Specifically, what has given the chain stores their buying superiority? Undoubtedly, one of the major reasons has been not only the ability to purchase in large quantities but to concentrate those purchases with one source or with a few suppliers. The chain store, by its specialization in certain lines of goods and its common practice of restricting its items to those in large demand, is able to give a manufacturer a contract for several months' or a year's supply instead of following the hand-to-mouth

buying practice which has been so common among independent
merchants. With a contract for a large order before him,
the manufacturer is able to figure his costs more closely
and at times to bring them down to extremely low levels.

To illustrate the matter of large purchases, the Woolworth organization in one year purchased ninety million
pounds of candy and twenty million pieces of enameled ware.
In another organization annual purchases from one biscuit
and cracker manufacturer amounted to more than ten million
dollars and there were other purchases of such amounts as
fifty million cakes of soap. A department store chain has
made annual purchases of four million handkerchiefs, six
million knitted undergarments, two and a half million men's
and boys' overalls, four and a half million men's and boy's
shirts, and two hundred thousand dozen pairs of women's hose.

In 1934 the Great Atlantic and Pacific Tea Company's
purchases from General Foods totaled about eight million dollars. The same company had a contract with the California
Packing Company for a definite purchase of two and a half
million cases of Del Monte label products at a five per cent
quantity discount. The Atlantic and Pacific actually took
during the time of the contract three and a half million
cases. Some idea of this enormous bargaining power may be
further had when it is considered that the Atlantic and
Pacific Tea Company makes total annual purchases amounting
to more than eight hundred million dollars and other chains
make purchases in proportionate amounts.

54

Since the quantity purchased vitally affects the price
paid, chains have secured reductions that were not usually
obtained by their independent competitors. Just how much
this buying advantage has contributed to chain store development is difficult to ascertain but the Federal Trade Commission studies have revealed that the proportion of the
chain grocery store price advantage represented by the buying
advantage varied from eighteen per cent to as high as forty-
five per cent in the four cities studied.

SKILLED BUYING.--In addition to securing economies
through the purchase of larger lots than are normally bought
by most wholesalers, chains employ skilled buyers and enjoy
the benefits of their specialization. Buyers with years of
training and experience in their particular field select just
the type of merchandise that will meet the desires of the
store's customers. The chain store depends on wise buyers to
choose out of hundred of items in any line the few best sellers. The chains know that the average customer bulks her
buying in towels or hosiery or lingerie at three or four
prices in each line, and therefore the chains, too, bulk
their merchandise investment and offerings at those prices.
The independent retailer without the same keen appreciation
of his customers' buying habits, may offer hosiery at thirteen
different prices, towels at ten prices, lingerie at eleven
prices, and yet miss completely one or two of the best price

lines in each group. Customers may prefer pink or blue,
but the independent retailer, unguided by expert headquarters opinion, offers her green which she rejects. It
must not be supposed that the above indictment is true of
all independent merchants but it is entirely too common
among the exponents of small-scale merchandising.

Expert chain store buyers, specializing in a very limited field, are able to keep in constant touch with the market and to take advantage of favorable opportunities as they
arise. Not only that, but their companies, by scientific
analysis, chemical tests, and other devices, can select merchandise on its merits and not by intuition or hearsay.

FINANCIAL STRENGTH.--Through their superior financial
resources, chains are generally able to pay cash for their
purchases whenever a favorable opportunity presents itself.
Many manufacturers when in need of ready money turn to chain
stores with offers of special discounts, and even though
chains do not always pay cash, they enjoy special consideration
because of their superior credit standing.

SPECIAL DISCOUNTS AND ALLOWANCES.--Perhaps the major
buying advantage which the chains have enjoyed in the past
has been the special discounts and allowances they have been
able to secure. That these more or less secret concessions
were a major factor in the development of the chain store has
long been suspected but it was not until the Federal Trade
Commission and the Patman Committee investigators brought out

the facts that their extent and magnitude became known. The
Federal Trade Commission study of 1930 revealed that in the
grocery trade, though the chain stores did but forty-four per
cent of the total retail grocery business, they secured ninety
per cent of the total special discounts and allowances granted,
wholesalers and cooperatives receiving the balance. The
special discounts and allowances which were granted were given
largely for volume purchases or for advertising. In the grocery trade, volume purchases allowances constituted forty-
three per cent of the total allowances made in 1930; advertising, forty-one per cent; and miscellaneous, sixteen per
cent. To suggest that these concessions were entirely unearned is hardly fair. Certainly at least part of the allowances for advertising was utilized by the chains for the
purposes for which they were intended, but the mere fact that
they were secret leads one strongly to suspect that they were
secured largely because of superior bargaining ability.

These secret concessions have enabled chains to secure
a competitive advantage over their independent rivals which
the latter have found difficult to overcome. When the total
volume of secret discounts and allowances is compared to total
retail sales volume, it may seem like an insignificant factor,
but when applied to specific items it is entirely another matter. For example, the Patman investigation revealed that in
the case of the Great Atlantic and Pacific Tea Company the
total secret allowances amounted to approximately $8,000,000

in 1934 or about one per cent of the total retail sales of
the company, which, when viewed casually, does not seem
like a major competitive factor. However, specific instances
present another picture. Take, for example, the case of one
prominent tea packer who allowed the company in cuestion an
extra ten cents per pound on all tea sold during a specific
period, or the yeast manufacturer who allowed this same chain
a flat monthly advertising allowance of twelve thousand dollars, at ten per cent quantity discount, and the usual jobber's discount. And these are not isolated cases; they appear
to be examples of common practices when selling to large-scale
buyers. After examining the list of manufacturers who granted
special prices to chains, one can understand more readily the
attitude of the independent merchant in clamoring for the enactment of the Robinson-Patman Bill. He felt that he was
helping subsidize the chain store through the higher prices
he was forced to pay to manufacturers so that the chains might
make his continuance in business more difficult, and he sought
legislation to remove that rather unfair advantage.

That the chains are entitled to certain special discounts
is not to be denied. For one thing, they do not practice
hand-to-mouth buying to a large extent; they make long-term
contracts with a manufacturer which enables him to use the
most economical type of machinery and turn out his product
on a decreasing cost basis. They do not require the manufacturer to carry spot stocks or employ expensive missionary
salesmen. One sales contact by the manufacturer's salesman

with a chain buyer will sell as much merchandise for him as
would several calls on wholesalers.

Chains enable the manufacturer readily to determine
consumer tastes and fancies. It is claimed that "all sorts
of complex investigations and surveys have failed to produce
an index of consumer demand that can approach in accuracy
and speed the trend of actual sales in a group of geograph-
ically diverse but individually similar retail stores."

But, it is claimed, wholesalers also do forward buying
and independent retailers also give point-of-sales promotional services and still they receive no special discounts
and allowances anywhere equal or proportionate to those received by chains. There is also a point beyond which quantity
purchases mean little or no additional savings to manufacturer.

Volume or promotional allowances are justified in so far
as they are based upon value received, and if the chains are
in a better position to give this service than the wholesaler
or independent retailer, then they are entitled to them. But
it seems that a large part of the allowances given is not
based on value received, but is tantamount to quoting a lower
price and takes the form of a rebate. It is a rather strange
situation for a manufacturer of well-known goods to have to
pay a chain organization to sell those goods when in reality
that is the purpose for which the chain is organized.

Under the Robinson-Patman Act which became law in June
1936, the chains are to be deprived of some of their unearned

allowances but only a "Pollyanna" would suggest that they
are to be stripped of them all. But it will probably be
some time before a chain can again secure better than fifty
per cent of its net profit from special discounts and allowances as the Great Atlantic and Pacific Tea Company did
in 1934.

CHAINS HAVE A LOW COST OF DOING BUSINESS.--The second
major advantage of the chain store is its ability to operate
at lower costs than its independent competitor, and it can
do this largely because of certain savings which it is able
to effect. The successful chains have foreseen the necessity for reduction of distribution costs and, by constant
vigilance as to expenses and the natural savings of mass operation, they have been able to widen profit margins and at
the same time reduce prices to the consumer. In 1929, for
which such complete data are extant, chain systems in the
grocery trade operated on a 17.3 per cent margin as contras-
ted with 24.7 per cent for the independent wholesaler--
retailer method.

INTEGRATION OF RETAILING WITH WHOLESALING.--Just what
savings have enabled chains to reduce operating costs?
First of all there is the savings due to the coordination
of wholesaling and retailing. By performing the functions
of both wholesaler and retailer the chain is able to effect
certain economies in operation that the ordinary wholesaler-
retailer channel of distribution has so far been unable to
achieve on any large scale. Few wholesalers can secure a

them to match the chain economies in getting physical goods
from warehouse to store. Except possibly in the case of
certain voluntary chains, this has been impossible. Again,
the chain does not have to sell its merchandise to individual
stores; it merely ships goods to them as needed and in that
way it escapes the heaviest item of the jobber's operating
expenses--an item that represents about twenty-five per cent
of its total operating costs. Neither does the chain incur
expense in extending credit or in collecting accounts, for
there are no dealings with outside customers except to a very
limited extent.

While no complete data for each type of business in
which chain stores operate are available, yet there can be
little doubt that the chain performs the jobber's functions
at considerably less cost than that incurred by general-line
service wholesalers. For example, in the grocery field the
1933 Census of American Business revealed that the cost of
doing business of general-line service wholesalers amounted
to 9.3 per cent of net sales, whereas the cost of doing business of chain store warehouses was but 4.3 per cent of net
sales. But the average chain store warehouse in the grocery
trade handles but approximately seventy per cent of the goods
billed through it. When allowance is made for this fact, the
cost of performing the wholesaling function on the part of
the chain store warehouses becomes approximately six per cent

rather than 4.3 Per cent. Even this larger figure represents
a considerable reduction in cost by comparison with regular
wholesalers. This reduction is brought about partly through
the curtailment of functions actually performed and partly
through more effective control and, perhaps, also through
more efficient performance of the remaining functions. In
this connection, it is interesting to note that if the independent retail grocer cares to patronize a cash-and-carry
wholesaler, he is able to secure his merchandise at lower
costs, for the operating expenses of such wholesalers are
also around six per cent. In addition to savings in wholesaling costs, the chain eliminates the wholesaler's net profit,
small as it may be, thereby bringing about an additional e-
conomy through integration.

LOWER SALARIES AND WAGES.--Chain store, through specialization in personnel and the use of relatively cheaper help
in their stores, are able to effect further operating economies. The Federal Trade Commission study revealed that in
each of the eight kinds of business furnishing comparable
data, the independent stores paid their employees substantially higher wages than did the chain stores. The table
on the following page clearly indicates this tendency of
the independent merchants to pay their employees more gen-
erously.

62

Table 8.--A Comparison of Chain and Independent Store Wages
of Full-Time Selling Employees for the Week Ending
January 10, 1931[1]

Type of Store	Average weekly wages independent employees	Average weekly wages chain employees	Averag net differ ences
Grocery and meat.........................	$25.90	$18.98	$6.92
Shoes....................................	33.48	27.83	5.65
Dry Goods................................	25.06	19.61	5.44
Drug.....................................	30.07	25.07	5.00
Grocery..................................	24.91	20.40	4.51
Ready-to-wear............................	31.11	27.77	4.34
Tobacco..................................	25.52	23.77	1.75
Hardware.................................	28.77	28.12	0.65
Total, simple average....................	28.10	23.82	4.28
Total, weighted average.................	28.48	21.61	6.87

This study embraces one thousand, five hundred and forty-
nine independent stores and fifty-five thousand, six hundred
and twenty-seven chain stores. A similar Federal Trade Com
mission study undertaken in thirty selected small towns ranging
in population from one thousand, seven hundred and thirty-
seven to five thousand, one hundred and six revealed that the
weekly wages of full-time selling employees of independent
merchants exceeded those of chain store employees by almost
three dollars.

63

Although both of these studies might be criticized because of the small sample, yet the fact that in practically every type of store studies, the chains paid their employees lower wages than their independent competitors seem clearly to indicate that the chain stores are effecting a material savings in wages. If further proof of this point is necessary, it may be found in the 1933 Census of American Business. According to this investigation the average annual earnings of full-time chain store employees was $1,079. The comparable figure of full-time independent employees amount to $1,194, if it is assumed that independent store proprietors are to be paid a thirty dollar weekly wage which is much lower than the average wage paid to managers of chain store units.

It is not the purpose of the authors to analyze at this point the social justice of the wages paid by chains or independents, but rather to bring out the point (and it is amply supported by factual evidence) that the chains are able to secure labor at lower costs than are their independent competitors. Part of this saving is due to their ability to use relatively cheaper help because of the standardized procedure developed at headquarters, part is probably due to the feeling that a large company offers more opportunities for promotion or that the job has more permanence than work with a small individual merchant, and part is due to their ability to specialize their functions so that each can be performed

so that each can be performed more economically. The cost of highly skilled and well paid experts can be spread over a number of units.

SMALLER INVENTORIES.--Another advantage of the chain is in inventory float, or in interest saved through a faster stock turnover. The chains confine themselves to standard merchandise for which there is a high average demand; they do not stock their shelves with slow-moving goods. A chain grocery store usually has from eight hundred to one thousand, and two hundred items, whereas most independent grocers carry from one thousand five hundred up to two thousand items.

FEWER SERVICES.--The chain store achieves further economies by limiting its services to the consumer. Chain stores have developed a reputation for doing a cash-and-carry business and, of course, everyone knows that is cheaper to do that kind of business than the full-service type. They have eliminated this cost without seriously inconveniencing their customers, because of the widespread use of automobiles, and few consumers stop to realize that they are assuming part of the middleman's function by carrying home their groceries themselves or by paying cash at time of purchase.

Just how prevalent the custom of eliminating services is among chain stores can be gathered from a study of the various lines of business in which chains operate. In eleven types of

business, including groceries and meat, drugs, and dry goods
apparel, ninety-five per cent of the sales are apparently
for cash.   In the lines which we generally associate with
chain stores (groceries, groceries and meat, drug) practically
all of the business is done on a cash basis.   Also the larger
chains were found to have eliminated more services than the
smaller ones.   For example, the organizations operating more
than one thousand stores did all their business on a cash
basis.   While the chains of two to five stores did only 43.4
per cent cash business.

The Federal Trade Commission reports that 80.8 per cent
of the chain stores of the United States gave no delivery
service or if they did it was negligible in amount, and in
the larger chains it was practically eliminated, since less
than one-half per cent of the sales of chains with more than
one thousand units were actually delivered.   However, in the
smaller chains, with six to ten stores each, the practice of
delivery was more prevalent, since thirty-eight per cent of
their sales were delivered.

Just how much is actually saved by the elimination of
these services?   In the year 1924, the Harvard Bureau of
Business Research found that one hundred and ten stores, all
with charge sales amounting to seventy-five per cent or more
of their total sales, commonly had a total expense (not including interest) amounting to 18.2 per cent as compared to

the corresponding figure of 14.55 per cent for forty-six
stores in each of which cash sales amounted to seventy-
eight per cent or more of total sales. The assumption is
that the stores selling for cash did not offer delivery
service to the same extent as stores selling for credit.
Thus there is a difference in cost of 3.65 per cent which may
be taken as fairly representative of delivery and credit extension cost. "There are grounds for believing that possibly
one-half of the expense savings realized by grocery chains as
compared to the wholesaler-retailer channel of distribution
accrue from the elimination or substantial reduction of these
services."

A more recent and undoubtedly conservative estimate of
the savings brought about by the elimination of services is
to be found in the data compiled by Dun & Bradstreet, Inc.,
in their "1936 Retail Survey." This study reveals that the
cost of rendering credit and delivery services is two per
cent in grocery stores and 2.4 per cent in combination grocery and meat stores. There are sound reasons for believing
that these figures are more truly representative of actual
conditions today than are earlier figures. However, Mr. Carl
W. Dipman, editor of PROGRESSIVE GROCER stated in July 1935,
"insofar as one can generalize it appears that credit service
when properly rendered need not add more than two per cent
to the operating expense, and, likewise, delivery service,

when properly and efficiently rendered, in general, need not
add more than two per cent, making a total of four per cent,
with three per cent representing a close approximation of actual conditions. Although the service saving will vary with
individual stores, it is readily apparent that this saving
affords the chain stores an important competitive cost advantage which they fully utilized.

BENEFITS OF STANDARDIZATION.--The ability of chain stores
to utilize standardization to its fullest extent has tended
further to reduce their operating costs. They have standardized their store fronts, displays, merchandise, policies, the
greetings of their salespeople, and they are still seeking
more factors to standardize. Chains do not leave to the
whims of the individual store managers, the working out of
displays or the selection of types of merchandise. These are
matters for the attention of highly skilled experts at the
home office, specialists whose sole duties are concerned with
the effective solution of each of these individual problems.
The interior of each unit of the apparel chain is decorated
in an attractive shade of pink whose reflective coloring has
been found to be flattering to most women. Had this been left
to the store manager perhaps he would have selected a ghastly
green whose unflattering atmosphere would have killed many a
sale. As far as possible the merchandise handled is standardized. Only those items that can be sold in volume are stocked.
They are applying the principle of mass production to merchandising, finding out what people want and then concentration

of their energies on those products follows the discovery.

SECONDARY BUSINESS ADVANTAGES.--Buying advantages and
low cost of operation are not the only advantages which have
played a major part in the development of chain stores. That
they possess certain advertising advantages, that they are
usually better financed, that they have superior facilities
for research and because of their size and reputation, that
they select their locations scientifically, and that they
have a superior ability for manufacturing and distributing
private brands are all matters to which most chains lay claim
to a certain extent over their typical independent competitor.
Practically all of these are inherently part of large-scale
merchandising and therefore are denied to most small owners.

Advertising has been classified here as a secondary advantage, not because it is unimportant, but rather because
it is less important than the two major advantages which
have been previously discussed. That chain stores have
marked advertising advantages over neighborhood unit stores
must be readily admitted. What individual small store operator can purchase large space in his city's daily news-
paper, broadcast regularly over the local radio station, or
purchase space in magazines of national reputation? The
waste circulation in any such venture would make the advertising cost prohibitive for the independent, but the chain
with its numerous units finds the same sort of advertising

economical. Individual merchants combining into voluntary
chains are able to achieve somewhat the same results but
even in this instance the chains occupy a favored position.

When the relative financial status of chains and independents is considered, we must once again recognize a definite balance in favor of the chains. With their large size,
their geographical distribution of risk, and their general
policy of selling for cash, chain stores find it a much easier
task to maintain strong, liquid financial positions than do
independents. If it becomes necessary to borrow money,
chains find that bankers are willing to lend at rates considerably under the rates the local merchant pays. One instance may be cited, as illustrative, where a chain borrowed
money for ninety days at one and a half per cent annual interest when local merchants of good financial reputation were
paying six per cent.

Chains operating a considerable number of units are able
to maintain a research department and to conduct experiments
on a scale and at a cost that is prohibitive to all but the
largest independent retailers. The best methods from the individual units can be adapted to all units of the system.
Various merchandising plans, store designs, displays, or advertising programs may be experimented with in one or several
units without danger of causing any serious loss to the organization as a whole. A novel type of store design can be
tried in one location and, if it proves successful, can be

adopted universally. An independent finds this sort of experimentation too precarious.

Owing to its very size, the chain secures a certain amount of prestige that helps draw patronage. Consumers become familiar with the chain name through advertising, through the financial and news columns of their local paper, in conversation with their friends, and from seeing various units of the chain in its many locations. It apparently is human nature to follow the crowd and the average individual assumes that because so many others trade at that particular chain store, perhaps they will also benefit by following suit.

Chain organizations are more careful in the location of their outlets than the average independent merchant. Large chains have separate real estate departments to select locations and to handle leasing and rentals. The selection of store sites has been made a scientific problem by chain real estate experts and guesswork has been reduced to a minimum. Traffic is not only counted but it is analyzed as to sex, purpose in passing, and buying power. Communities are studied as to character of population, type and stability of industries, local buying habits, and strength of competition. When a chain store settles upon a definite location, it usually has a good estimate of the volume of business it may expect. Few independents have access to the same type of impartial information on store sites.

71

Some chains are able to manufacture and distribute successfully their own privately branded merchandise, and today, more than ever before, this appears as a distinct advantage. With some forty-odd states having filed fair-trade laws in operation and with the Robinson-Patman Act in effect, the savings that chains are able to achieve through manufacturing their own merchandise appear particularly timely. Specifically the reasons chains have given for engaging in manufacturing are that it enables them to control sources of supply, that they can secure their goods at lower cost, that they can sell at lower prices, that they give consumers better values, and that they can partially circumvent some of the more recent types of legislation which they regard as discriminatory. However, the advantages of manufacturing their own products are not available to all. Only those chains which do a large volume business in specific lines can manufacture profitably. This is especially true of apparel and of the larger food and drug chains.

ECONOMIC ADVANTAGES OF CHAIN STORE OPERATION.--In addition to the purely business advantages which chain stores possess, they have certain inherent economic advantages which are not generally enjoyed by smaller retail institutions. These advantages arise principally out of the peculiar economic nature of business. Certain enterprises are able to profit to a better degree than some competitors merely because of our highly developed economic structure.

72

RISK DISTRIBUTION.--One of the most obvious economic
advantages is the one involving the distribution of risk.
As the chain generally operates units over a wide geographical area, it is not necessarily dependent on any one community for its prosperity. If local business conditions
are bad in one locality, the profits from stores operated
in more prosperous areas will help offset the losses in
the former. The independent merchant, on the other hand,
is much more seriously affected by local conditions since
he has only his own community to depend on for his success.
This same width of market enables chain stores to transfer
slow-moving stock from some of their stores to units in
which the demand for such goods is very much greater.

CHAIN MERCHANDISING IS ONE OF DECREASING COSTS.--One
of the fundamental reasons for chain store success lies in
the simple fact that "it is more economical to run two stores
than it is to run one, that it is more economical to operate
one hundred stores than ten, that it is more economical to
operate one thousand stores than one hundred, and so on."
Economies are effected by adding units so that costs can
be spread over a larger volume of business. Of course, not
all chains can operate on a decreasing cost basis, but it
does seem that many do. We do know that as more units are
added to a productive combination, the time will come when
the average return per unit will begin to decrease, and if
too many units are added, the time will come when net profits

begin to decrease. Few chain store operators admit that
their chain has reached the point of diminishing returns,
and an inspection of chain store profits will reveal the
reason. An examination of the data in the next table reveals quite clearly that in the majority of cases the percentage of net profit for the larger chains is greater than
it is for the smaller ones. The one-dollar-limit variety
chains are a good example. The net operating profit in
this line climbs from 2.81% for chains of two to five stores
until it averages 10.47% for chains of more than one thousand
units. Of course, not all of the larger chains are able
to net more profit than the smaller ones, but many factors
such as variations in managerial skill, territorial differences, etc., would account for these deviations. The
significant fact is that in most instances the larger chains
are able to earn a substantially higher rate of net profit.

Some may wonder why operating expenses instead of
net profits were not used to substantiate the assertion
that chain retailing is essentially a business of decreasing costs. However, a true picture of the situation can
not be secured from an inspection of expenses alone. The
available statistics (or at least the Federal Trade Commission reports) include all chain costs, and, as the larger
chains engage more extensivly in their own wholesaling and
manufacturing, their expenses include costs which are not

incurred by the smaller chains. If it were possible to dif-
ferentiate the various expense, then comparable data could
be secured.

PERCENTAGE OF NET PROFIT TO SALES, BY SIZE OF CHAIN

Kind of Chain	Number of Store per Chain								
	2-5	6-10	11-25	26-50	51-100	101-500	501-1000	1001 and over	Average
Confectionery.....	2.53	6.57	8.48	7.95	1.44	11.21	....	....	6.04
Drug..............	2.91	4.03	4.41	4.13	4.38	4.92	2.49	....	4.21
Dry Goods and Ap.	13.41	4.34	3.64	0.14	4.52	8.56	7.43	5.72	5.93
Grocery..........	2.15	1.66	1.52	1.66	1.93	2.63	1.68	2.23	2.10
Grocery and Meat..	1.98	1.91	1.68	2.22	2.04	1.86	2.42	2.98	2.82
Men's and Women's shoes.....	4.95	1.63	2.55	2.86	0.94	4.19	....	....	3.17
Millinery........	2.84	2.00	2.44	1.51	1.97	2.90	....	....	2.36
Tobacco..........	1.37	0.25	0.30	1.34	0.32	3.79	....	2.60	2.68
Variety ($1 limit)	2.81	3.20	6.17	6.58	4.49	8.60	9.75	10.47	9.16
Women's ready-to-wear...	2.53	5.71	3.12	5.56	4.97	4.37	....	....	4.35
Women's Shoes....	.97	1.24	4.08	2.42	6.77	7.59	....	....	3.48

Another point that bears out the assertion that chain
retailing is one of decreasing costs is that the courts have
quite generally given their approval to graduated license
taxes. By legalizaing this tax the courts have placed their

tacit stamp of approval on the principle of increasing returns for chains with increases in the number of units. The
courts have repeatedly held tnat chain stores possess advantages and opportunities not possessed by single-store operators and that the larger chains possess them to greater degree
than the smaller ones. In The West Virginia chain store tax
decision the United States Supreme Court said, " A chain is
a distinctive business species, with its own capacities and
functions. Broadly speaking, its opportunities and powers
become greater with the number of component units, and the
greater they become the more far reaching are the consequences,
both social and economic."

Varying Prices.--One very important economic advantage
of chain store operation is the ability to vary prices, not
only within the same city but between different sections of
the country. The chain is able to average their profit results from those obtained from the different stores, the high
profits accrued in one section of stores offsetting the low
returns from another group of stores. It may charge what
the traffic will bear or what competition will allow.

Few of the chains interviewed by representatives of the
Federal Trade Commission kept strict control of competitive
prices from headcuarters but gave some store managers and
district officials authority in this matter, thus giveing to
these people a strong competitive weapon. Chain store officials indicated"...that it is a ouite usual practice among

them to cut prices locally not only to meet, but to go below, the prices of their competitors in that locality, while maintaining prices in their other stores."

Out of five hundred and thirty seven reasons given for price variation by four hundred and one intersectional and intercity chains, about thirty-six per cent of the reasons were to the effect that competition was the cause for such a policy. In the case of one hundred and forty-two intercity chains, 37.5 per cent of the reasons cited competition as the cause for a varying price policy within the same city while about eleven per cent, the second highest percentage, were based on the difference in class of customers or neighborhood.

A representative from the Great Atlantic and Pacific Tea Company, testifying before the Patman Investigating Committee on July 9, 1935, stated that the two factors in deciding the company's retail prices were cost and competition. He stated that his organization felt that they must undersell the independent to the extent of the service in respect to credit extention and delivery which the latter gives.

Some may say that this is all very good and true, but since the chain has many outlets and independent has only one, the chain encounters competition at many more places and many more times than does the independent and therefore this ability to average prices means little in the way of an advantage. Of course, there is truth to this, but it

lessens the advantage very little. Price cutting is of
great significance to the independent, or small chain for
that matter, because it affects his total business, and
thus means much more to the smaller than the larger competitors. It is not likely that all the units of a large
chain will be engaged in price wars at the same time.
This averaging process is one advantage that the cooperative or voluntary chain cannot attempt to attain for its
members.

A certain chain organization with an average investment of $969,000 over a period of years in the Cincinnati
territory "...had an annual loss of considerably more than
their total investment in that territory while they were
driving the independents out of business." From 1930 to
1933, the same organization had an average investment of
$813,250 in Los Angeles, California," .....and an actual
loss during those years of $862,918." In the year 1926
and 1927 this organization's loss in Dallas, Texas, was
fifty thousand dollars more than its capital investment,"
...whereas in other cities in this country it showed that
at the same time, where they had got control, as in the
Bronx, in New York, they made as much as one hundred and
fifty per cent on their capital invested; and in other
cities in this country, where they had complete control
and set the prices, they made enormous profits." Thus the
profits of other stores may be used by the chain for price
cutting any other locality.

78

SUMMARY OF CHAIN STORE ADVANTAGES.--In summarizing the advantages which chain stores possess, it would seem that they center largely around the result of scientific retailing which can best be attempted when merchandise is distributed in volume. That chain stores as a group operate more efficiently than their ordinary independent competitors as a group has been proved by practically every comparative price or cost study that has covered these factors. This ability to undersell is the direct result of certain advantages which are inherent in chain store merchandising. Among the business advantages are the vitally important ability to buy cheaply, the facility to operate at low costs, and certain secondary advantages, such as advertising, financial resources, and others. Among the economic advantages which are partially responsible are the dispersion of risks, the decreasing cost nature of the business, and the opportunity to vary prices to meet local conditions.

Though some of the advantages mentioned above are denied the independent merchant, most of them are available to aggressive small-scale merchandisers who choose to use them. By applying the same principles of scientific retailing and by utilizing group buying, the independent can secure the major advantages which the chain possesses. That they have taken their cue from the chain

store and are adopting large-scale retailing principles to
their own businesses seems readily apparent. A glance
through the comparative price studies made during the past
several years reveals a very definite trend in the diminishing size of the price differential between chain-store
and independent-store prices. For example, the earliest
grocery investigation found a price difference of more than
ten per cent in favor of the chains, but the latest study
of the same line of trade reveals less than a five per cent
differential. That this is indicative of the declining
importance of chain store advantages is a reasonable assumption.

Some of the advantages which chain stores possess might
be termed unfair. Certainly chain store operators are open
to criticism, for having paid their employees less than independent operators did, and it is not to their credit that
they have clubbed manufacturers into selling them goods at
unfair discounts. It is only a question of time before
the chain store will be deprived of these unfair advantages,
and even when this does happen, it will still require a
very efficient independent merchant to compete successfully
against the legitimate advantages which the chain will
always possess.

VI

DISADVANTAGES OF CHAIN STORES

80

CHAIN STORE DISADVANTAGES AND LIMITATIONS.--To the
vast majority of the American public the chain store has
appeared as a new form of business colossus destined to
replace the independent merchant. This apparently invincible business giant whose invasion of the retailing field
seemed so successful some few years ago has been found to
have pregnable armor. No longer does the intelligent independent look to the future with dismay, for he knows
that the further progress of chains is beset with numerous
obstacles. The chain system has developed several serious
disadvantages, and certain limiting factors have appeared
to impede its further growth. Not that chain stores have
suddenly found themselves face-to-face with insurmountable
obstacles. Such is definitely not the case. Rather the
chains have discovered that they, too, are subject to many
natural disadvantages of other large-scale retailing institutions and in addition suffer from several special disadvantages. These have all tended to curb the rapid progress
of chain stores and it is not beyond the realm of possibility
that they may actually cause a decline in the relative importance of this form of retailing. As yet, however, these
disadvantages have not proved a definite barrier to further
progress; instead they are merely slowing up chain store
growth.

In the discussion of chain store weaknesses which follows, nothing will be done to attempt to distinguish between

disadvantages and limitations on the ground that fundamentally they tend to have essentially similar effects. Both definitely tend to check chain store progress. Again, no attempt will be made to discuss the economic or social disadvantage of chain stores.

CHAIN MERCHANDISING NOT ADAPTABLE TO ALL TYPES OF GOODS.--A study of the chain store situation reveals the fact that this system of merchandising is not equally adaptable to all lines of retailing. Despite the progress chain stores have made in retailing generally, there are certain fields in which they have found it difficult to operate successfully. For example, in the hardware and jewelry trades they do but a very small share of the total volume, whereas in the variety store sphere they have virtually eliminated the independent merchant.

It is not so much that certain types of business have been overlooked by chains, but rather that certain kinds of retailing are less susceptible to the chain method of operation. Where a great diversity of items must be handled as in hardware, difficulties are encountered. Minute care and supervision are necessary in order to maintain a balanced stock and carelessness on the part of the local manager may result in a serious lack of essential items or in excessive inventories of unsalable or slow moving merchandise.

82

Further difficulties are found in those businesses which require considerable discretion on the part of individual store managers and which do not readily lend themselves to extensive standardization. To entrust responsibility and authority extensively to unit managers is something that chains ordinarily shun. In lines of trade without definite price schedules or with multiple-price systems, chains find it particularly difficult to operate successfully. The same is true of trades in which contract work prevails, as each contract offers a particularized pricing problem and complicated sales promotion and installation duties.

LACK OF PERSONAL CONTACT WITH CUSTOMERS.--Like other large-scale retailers, chain stores suffer disadvantages in the lack of personal contact between their management and the public. A chain store patron rarely comes in contact with the owners and major executives of the business and his relations with the store are confined to meetings with the rank and file of subordinate employees. Even though those workers, because of a desire for promotion or to retain their jobs, and with a certain amount of training and supervision, may produce some measure of efficiency, they, nevertheless, usually function with less effectiveness than do the owners of small businesses with their sharpened personal interest in customers. It is the

age-old principle of self-interest stimulating individual
initiative to produce effective results. An owner naturally takes more interest in the welfare of his customers than
does a hired worker.

The independent store has an individuality which is
largely a reflection of the personality of its owner. This
characteristic may be friendly, it may be cold, it may be
good, or it may be bad, but, whatever else it is, it is distinctive. The chain, oh the other hand, has a standardized,
corporate personality which undoubtedly appeals to many, but
its impersonal character does not attract consumers to the
same extent that the independents' distinctiveness does.

The independent merchant usually realizes that he must
serve his individual customers as they wish to be served or
his entire business existence is imperiled. The chain
store manager, on the other hand, feels that even though the
success of his particular store may be of considerable importance to his own career, the success or failure of the
chain is not dependent upon the accomplishments of this one
single unit. Customers are often aware of the attitude and
appreciate the individual attention the independent merchant
can give them. Quite frequently, however, the independent
merchant interprets his designation too literally and acts
much too independent toward his customers. On this score,
they must be severely criticized, although as a class they
do not deserve the criticism.

84

Chains are at a disadvantage when competing with independents, as their competition of management must be by
proxy. The independent-store manager operates directly and
is in personal contact with his business, whereas chain-
store management experts must act indirectly through assis-
tants. The value of the experts' work is almost certain to
lose some of its quality and inspiration as it flows outward
through the mechanism of the organization.

RELATIVE INFLEXIBILITY OF CHAIN MERCHANDISING.--Closely akin
to the lack of personal contact is the relative inflexibility
of chain stores. Chain merchandising is essentially based on
the principle of standardization. Store fronts, equipment,
merchandise, advertising, services, and even selling are all
standardized. This uniformity has its virtues and certain
economies are effected thereby, but at the same time the
chains find it difficult to adapt themselves to local conditions as readily as the independent merchant can. The latter
makes his store, his policies, and his merchandise fit the
needs of those whom he seeks to serve. If he is in the grocery business, he may handle almost any brand of merchandise
his particular customers may desire or offer them the type
of service that he knows will appeal to them. But can the
chain store manager do the same? Hardly! He is permitted
some leeway, of course, but he is apt to be confined to the
particular brands that sell best in other stores of the chain,
and, in the matter of service, he will probably find himself

limited to that which can be rendered effectively by all
of the organizations' units, although some notable exceptions to this may now be found.

The distance between the consumer and the chain executives who determine management policy makes it necessary to operate on a highly standardized basis in order to
effect those economies which are necessary to chain store
success. That standardization has its virtues is obvious
and in order to secure those advantages chain stores have
found it necessary to sacrifice a certain amount of flex-
ibility. In some lines of business this lack of adapta-
bility has proved to be a distinct impediment to the progress
of chains. This has been especially true of the shopping
and specialty goods fields. Chains have made rapid strides
in those fields only since they sacrificed some of the
standardization, placed more responsibility in and allowed
more discretion to the individual store managers. However,
in certain lines of business, as in groceries, where high-
priced unit managers would prove too costly, only limited
discretion can be given to such managers; hence the relative
inflexibility becomes an inherent part of chain management
in such lines of trade.

PERSONNEL PROBLEMS.--One of the most pressing problems
facing the chains is that of personnel and employee morale.
As the chain organization grows in size, the personnel problem becomes increasingly complex. More and more the work of

the organization must be carried on by subordinate employees.
The management is forced to delegate a larger share of responsibility and authority to minor executives, and the
skill with which the latter may perform these duties may
well determine the ultimate success of the enterprise.

Scientific selection, training, and supervision of
chain store employees become a virtual necessity for successful merchandising. It becomes increasingly important
to have each worker carefully selected from the applicants
for his job and then properly trained in his duties. This
condition makes it necessary to expand considerably the
functions and facilities of the personnel department. The
expense of conducting training programs for store managers
and other employees rises and, in companies with high rates
of labor turnover, the costs are likely to become excessive.
If a store manager leaves to work for a competitor or to
operate an independent store, the benefits of his training
are largely dissipated, at least from the viewpoint of his
previous employers. From a social and economic point of
view, however, as will be shown in a later statement, there
is a decided gain from this training and to that extent the
chain method of merchandising has contributed to the growing
efficiency in retail merchandising.

Furthermore, as the chain continues to grow, it becomes
ever increasingly difficult to inculcate the spirit of a-
chievement in employees. In an enormous organization an

employee will begin to feel that he does not have an even
chance for advancement and that wage increases are dependent
largely upon things other than his own ability and achieve-
ments. There are many store managers who feel, however, that
they are destined for, and capable of achieving greater things
than their present position holds for the, although they may
be definitely limited in their abilities. It is this problem of keeping such individuals satisfied, and yet ambitious,
that the chains must continue to face in the future. Partly
on this account and partly because of the relatively limited
economic opportunities certain chains have adopted the policy
of hiring individuals with average abilities. For example,
some chains seldom hire from among college graduates the
students who proved to possess superior qualities in schol-
arship or campus leadership.

Another phase of the personnel problem that the chains
find handicaps them is that it becomes increasingly difficult to fill satisfactorily the higher executive positions
in the organization. In a small organization the functions
are simple and employees holding responsible positions find
it comparatively easy to perform their duties well. As the
organization grows, these same functions become vastly more
complex and, in many instances, the job has completely out-
grown the man. For example the store manager may be able
to do a highly satisfactory job in that capacity but when

promoted to managership of a group of stores in a given
district, he may find himself unable to perform his new
functions, satisfactorily and to cope with his problems
as an executive with vision and foresight should.

PROBLEMS OF HANDLING STYLE GOODS.--It is frequently
said that fashion goods cannot be merchandised centrally
and therefore, can never amount to much in a chain way.
Many a chain store antagonist has been whistling in the
dark by saying that "you can't chain fashion. You can't
buy hats like hair pins, nor evening wraps like eggs.
You can't merchandise dresses centrally. No buyer in New
York can select style goods for stores in other cities.
Every store is different and every city is different.
Maybe, you can buy bedding centrally, but not apparel."
But it is being done, and being done successfully, profitably, and increasingly. We find that fifty per cent of the
shoe store business and 25.5 per cent of the women's ready-
to-wear store volume were done by chains in 1935. In both
of these lines the chains registered a substantial gain
over 1929.

That it is more difficult for chain organizations to
handle fashion goods than convenience goods is undoubtedly
true. It is not an easy task for the central office to determine accurately the merchandise needs of the individual
retail units, which may vary with local tastes. Nor is it
a simple matter to place responsibility for unsatisfactory

results when the purchase of goods is separated from the
sale. Department and individually operated specialty
stores generally find it necessary to combine the functions
of purchase and sale in order to secure efficient merchandising. The chains have met this difficulty by shifting
more responsibility to the individual store managers. In
some cases they have given such managers more freedom in
the selection of goods by allowing them to choose their
merchandise from a range of patterns and styles contracted
for by the central buying office. In other instances
representatives from the purchasing office call on store
managers with a line of samples from which selections for
the individual stores are made. Some of the chains operating large units have found it advisable to have each store
do its own buying. Furthermore, with the greater use of
automobiles and the more frequent attendance of motion pic-
tures, the distinction in styles in different sections of
the country and in varying-sized communities is fast dis-
appearing. Not only there is a tendency for people throughout the country to be influenced by the same style of merchandise, but also to adopt the same style simultaneously.
Whatever style lag still exists is rapidly diminishing in
importance. All this plays into the hands of the chains.

Another difficulty chain stores are facing in the
handling of style merchandise is in price reductions.
Style obsolescence or local competitive conditions may

make it necessary to reduce prices very promptly. Chain
Stores, with their concentration of authority, frequently
find it inconvenient to act speedily in such cases and
serious losses may occur as a result of the delay or from
the necessity of having the central office act without an
adequate knowledge of local conditions, unless such matters
become solely the prerogative of the unit managers.

Style goods, more than any other type of merchandise,
must be adapted to the desires of a store's patrons. Because of their inherent nature, chain stores should be at
a disadvantage when competing with independents in fashion
lines. However, as indicated above, that has not been the
case, largely because they have attempted to locate their
units in communities where the customers and their problems
are nearly identical and because of the other factors previously indicated. They have certainly made progress in
these fields, and so it may be truthfully stated that the
difficulties of merchandising style goods by chain stores
have been considerably overrated in the past.

ASSOCIATION WITH PRICE MERCHANDISING.--Almost from
the date of their origin chain stores have been merchandising price. In their advertising, in merchandise stocks,
and in selling methods they have emphasized the price appeal.
They have helped foster a price consciousness in the mind
of the American consumer which does not always react to

their own advantage. Although low price does not necessarily infer that the merchandise is of inferior quality,
still the public generally feels that it may have to sac-
riflee quality, style, or some other feature in return for
the savings resulting from paying reduced prices. This has
not proved to be a material handicap to chains in the con-
venience-goods field. But in certain lines of trade and
among some classes of consumers this does prove to be a
stumbling block. In the upper price levels of the apparel
field consumers are less responsive to the price appeal and
that is one reason that the chains have not made more progress in that sphere.

Another disadvantage resulting from a price emphasis
is that trade bounds to a store because of this appeal is
usually not very securely tied to that particular store.
Persons seeking bargains are readily lured from store to
store in their quest for maximum values. They continue to
patronize their favorite stores only so long as they feel
that no other store is offering better "buys."

As long as chain stores are able to maintain their
price advantage through their ability to buy for less or
to operate at lower cost, and emphasis on cost is frequently a decided advantage in drawing trade from competing establishments. As they lose this ability to sell
for less (and they are losing some of it through improved
efficiency among independents and as a result various types

of legislation) then the bargain atmosphere surrounding
many chain stores becomes less appealing to consumers.
It then becomes necessary to compete with independents
along lines in which the latter are less handicapped,
such as quality, service, convenience, and personality.

LACK OF SERVICE.--While the elimination of services
such as the extension of credit and delivery reduces chain
store costs, at the same time it has the effect of limiting
patronage. Many consumers feel that they would rather enjoy
these services than save a few pennies by going without them.
There are many others, on the other hand, who feel inclined
to visit retail stores, pay cash, and bring home their own
purchases in order to effect these same economies. The widespread use of automobiles has encouraged consumers to patronize cash-and-carry stores, but there is still a vast
body of them who balk at the inconvenience caused by lack
of service, especially credit and delivery.

Not all chain stores have eliminated services. On the
contrary, in lines such as jewelry, clothing, and furniture,
they feature all the services normally rendered yearly by
independents, and many even go beyond by offering unusually
liberal credit accommodations. Nor is the extension of service limited to those businesses. Only recently it was discovered that fifty per cent of the chain grocery stores in
highly competitive centers like New York and Boston are

extending either delivery or credit service to their customers.

When chain stores extend services they naturally increase their costs and lessen their ability to undersell
the independent. The higher the costs go, the more likely
they are to lose their price advantage over independent
stores. It is hardly possible that an effective price appeal can be coupled with the expenses incident to the extension of services.

ANTAGONISTIC PUBLIC OPINION.--In the past few years
the chain stores have encountered hostility on the part of
the public. Some of this has been engendered by the vicious
attacks of certain individuals who have seen it an opportunity to further their own personal interests; some has been
due to sentiment aroused by their independent competitors,
and some is just part of the natural prejudice which the
public apparently feels toward big business.

Various and sundry charges have been leveled against
chain stores, some of which are without foundation in fact,
but which have, nevertheless, had their effect on the public
mind. Chain stores have endured attacks from many quarters
which have had some detrimental effect on their volume of
business. A poll conducted by the Institute of Public Relations in 1936 revealed that about seventy per cent of the
persons interviewed felt that chain stores should be leg-
islated against in one form or another. To few others in

business is attached the stigma in the public mind from
which the chains suffer.

Some of this ill will has been due undoubtedly to
chain store practices. Chains were slow to realize that
they had a public realations problem to solve. It was not
until the latter part of the twenties that they began to
donate extensively to charitable organizations and partake
in movements for community betterment. Recently certain
chains, notably the S. S. Kresge Company and Montgomery Ward,
have adopted the policy of active participation in local
activities. The chains are not beginning any too soon to
realize that there is more to merchandising and distribution of goods than mere price appeal. As a matter of fact,
they must build good will in the eyes of the public for
self-protection. They are now showing a tardy appreciation
of the value of favorable public opinion and many of them
are actively engaged in wooing the public.

GROWING COMPETITION.--In the early part of their expansion, chain stores encountered little opposition from
the average independent. Apparently, merchants were de-
moralized by this new retail titan. But it was not long
before the independent merchants awakened to the need for
fighting back. They found that by adopting chain store
methods they could compete more effectively. As the
weaker merchants were driven out of business the stronger

ones survived, and the general level of competitive ability among independent merchants was raised. Independents were not slow in discovering that they could profitably adopt efficient chain store practices: stores were cleaned up; windows decorated; and retail clerks trained. Superfluous brands, price lines, and sizes were reduced or eliminated. Better display methods and advertising practices were adopted. The chain stores are now finding that the 1937 independent is not the same independent they encountered then, ten or fifteen years ago.

The independents have met chain competition in still another way, by joining cooperative buying organizations. Realizing that one of the major chain store advantages was that of buying, independents banded together in buying groups and in voluntary chains in an effort to secure their merchandise at costs comparable to those obtained by the chains. Potentially, such organizations have the ability to place the independents on a merchandising par with chains. In fact, it is entirely possible that with the advantages of personal initiative, ambition, ownership, intimate customer contacts, added services, and similar superior characteristics, the corporate chains may be hard pressed to maintain their position.

Not only are the chains faced with increased competition from the more intelligent and well-organized independents, but they are beginning to feel the intense

competition of other chains. The chains have been spread-
ing rapidly in the face of independent opposition, but in
many lines they have reached the point where their major
competition is now coming from other multiple-store groups.
It is a much more difficult problem now that they face competitors who possess inherently all of their own advantages.
The financial difficulties of some chains and the diminishing
profits of others in the last few years give ample evidence
of the increasing competition that chains are encountering
among themselves. It has indeed become a battle of giants.

Another competitive situation facing chain stores is
that of overlapping lines carried by chains presumably in
other fields. The drug stores are carrying grocery items
and in some cases even wearing apparel, and in retaliation
the grocery chain stores have placed patent medicines on
their shelves and frequently have installed soda fountains.
Certainly, the variety stores have encroached upon the restaurant, dry goods, department, and grocery chain fields.

Recently, chain stores have begun to encounter a newer
and more invincible type of competition. The rapid expansion of supermarkets in the food field has presented serious
difficulties for the grocery and meat chains and has even
affected the drugs. Possessing a lower cost of doing business and offering a wider selection of merchandise than one
commonly finds in chain food stores, this new competition
is proving formidable. Supermarkets have a cost advantage

due largely to self-service and low rentals which enable
them to save probably one-third of the operating expenses
of the average chain food store. This new type of competition has been probably the primary factor in inducing
chains to open larger stores of their own and also actually
adopting the supermarket method of operation.

LEGISLATIVE HANDICAPS.--Many problems in the form of
legislative restrictions are also plaguing the chains today. Special taxes have been levied against them, their
buying advantages have been curtailed by the Robinson-Patman Act, their price advantage has been lessened by state
fair-trade laws, and now increased surplus taxes are restricting their ability to expand.

In twenty states chain store taxes are now in effect.
These taxes vary from a few dollars to five hundred and
fifty dollars per unit per year, as is the case in Lou-
isiana. In practically every instance the tax imposed is
a graduated tax which increases with the number of stores;
for example, the Michigan Act taxes the first two stores
ten dollars; the next three twenty-five dollars each; the
next five one hundred dollars each; and all stores in excess of twenty-five pay two hundred and fifty dollars each.
In the case of Idaho all stores over nineteen pay five hundred dollars a year each. The principle of graduated chain
store license taxes has been declared constitutional by the

98

United States Supreme Court and the chains are finding it
increasingly difficult to fight this restriction on their
business. As long as the taxes are not excessive, they do
not curtail chain store expansion, but in many cases they
are proving a serious burden in the filling station and grocery fields. Few chain filling stations can afford to pay
the two hundred and fifty dollar license tax which the state
of West Virginia levies nor can the smaller units of grocery
chains in Idaho well afford to pay the five hundred dollar
tax which that state exacts.

As long as there is crying need for revenue, combined
with the pressure from independent retailer and wholesaler
groups, chain store taxes will probably be extended rather
than curtailed. To date they have not seriously handicapped
chain stores except in certain states and in lines of business
where the profit or sales per unit are small. The tendency,
however, is for the chain store tax to increase their efficiency and meet the independents on more even ground. It
may be possible then that the taxes will be an important
limiting factor in further chain expansion.

One of the most recent bits of legislation to hamper
the chain store has been the Robinson-Patman Law which reduces some of the buying advantages of chains. Under the
provisions of this act, as it is now being enforced, the
chains are finding it difficult to secure the same special
discounts and allowances which they have enjoyed in the past.

99

Should they be materially deprived of this advantage,
they will find it increasingly difficult to undersell
the independent merchant.

The speed with which the state legislatures have
enacted fair-trade laws may soon make it extremely difficult for chain stores to undersell independents on
nationally branded items. Some forty-two states now have
fair-trade laws in effect, and it is expected that a total of forty-four states will soon have such laws on their
statute books. As the chain stores are deprived of their
price weapon, their ability to compete against the up-to-
date independent will proportionally diminish.

In the past, chain stores have financed their expansion
largely through the reinvestment of their earnings. With
the new Federal legislation which taxes reinvested earnings
at a higher rate than earnings paid out in dividends, it
will be more difficult for chains to expand in that fashion.
Stockholders will naturally clamor for a distribution of
earnings in the form of cash dividends. This, of course,
will tend to limit the desire for expansion, or at least
it will make the policy of expansion more expensive than
it has previously been.

VII

HOW INDEPENDENTS ARE TRYING TO
COMBAT AND COMPETE WITH CHAINS

100

Voluntary Chains and Combinations of Independents.--
At the present time it is estimated that there are three
hundred and seventy-five cooperative merchandising, advertising and buying groups controlling fifty-five thousand independent grocery stores or virtually matching the
grocery chain organizations in number of units operated.
The growth of these so-called voluntary chains of retail
grocers has been astounding. There are also a number of
similar voluntary chains in the drug field and McKesson
and Robbins have found a huge merger of drug wholesalers
to perform a service somewhat similar to these cooperatives.
The advantages accruing to the voluntary chain movement are
many where there has been a substantial revamping of and
control over stores and methods by the managing wholesaler
or central association. The advantages insure lower prices
and the exploitation of a "leader policy." Stores are
taught cleanliness, attractive arrangement and layout, and
standardization of stock. To a certain extent these voluntary chains have private brands of their own which it is
easier to develop because of the greater amount of personal
salesmanship of the individual proprietor.

Service motives.--As has been shown, personal service
in the chain store from clerk to customer is conspicuous
by its absence. Independent dealers are using this fault
of the chain store to their own advantage. Helpful advice

to the customer making a purchase is a valuable asset and
is always appreciated by the prospective customer. This
personal contact problem is of great importance,is being
used by the independent dealers to offset other chain-
store advantages, among which service is limited if not
negligible.

VIII

ARGUMENTS AGAINST CHAIN STORES

102

Many arguments have been presented both in favor of
and opposed to chain stores. The following are the arguments given on the question. First, the arguments against
chains------

I Chain Stores Have Created A State Of Confusion In The
   Field Of Distribution.

    a. They have threatened the stability of certain
       manufacturing concerns.

    b. They are undertaking the functions of jobbers
       and wholesalers.

    c. Chains are making it harder for the independent
       retailer to stay in business.

    d. Chain stores confuse the public regarding market
       price of standard trade-branded goods.

    e. The system creates temptation to resort to short
       weights and measures to souare daily sales reports.

    f. Chains do not give the type of service offered by
       independent stores.

    g. Chains often advertise one price and sell at another.

    h. Chain store clerks are not trained to give to the
       customers helpful service.

II Danger of Monopoly

    a. They carry such a large variety of articles they
       need not depend on any single line to obtain
       volume turnover.

b. Some of the leading chain-stores executives predict their system will eventually control ninety per cent of the retail trade.

c. Already the trend toward concentration of ownership is evident.

d. Concentration of ownership creates a tendency toward mergers.

e. There is a growing tendency for chains to join control of the manufacturing industry.

III Chain Stores Produce Certain Harmful Social Reactions.

a. Rapid expansion of chains threatens the well-being of small business.

b. Chains have limitations in business operation which give the public certain disadvantages.

c. Chain stores take no responsibility for the welfare of the community.

d. The chain system takes from us opportunities for personal satisfaction.

e. Chain stores are contributing to an already serious labor problem.

IX

ARGUMENTS FOR CHAIN STORES

104

I   Chain Stores give the public advantages of sound economic
methods of distribution which they have introduced.

    a.   They have eliminated delivery service and
credit accounts, thereby reducing overhead
expenses.

    b.   They have adopted methods of scientific mass
buying.

    c.   Improved methods of accounting and inventory.

    d.   Quick turnover improves quality of their stock
by eliminating perishable goods.

    e.   Greater efficiency per person than other stores
due to fact that chain store managers must prove
their productive ability.

    f.   System of self service and automatic buying where-
by customer sells himself through the proper display of merchandise.

    g.   The scientific and improved methods of distribution
as introduced by chain stores have been beneficial
to independent retailers.

II The Present status of chain stores does not point toward
a dangerous monopolistic control of the retail field.

    a.   They appear to have reached the limits of profit-
able expansion.

    b.   Chains do only nineteen per cent of the entire
retail business.

c. Chains will find it more difficult to expand in the future.

d. Chains never intended to drive independent re-tailers completely from field of distribution.

e. The fact that small capital of independent finds it hard to compete with large capital is not a violation of business ethics.

f. Chain Store Taxation.

III Chain stores contribute to the general social and economic well-being of the public.

a. Help eliminate waste in field of distribution.

b. Prices lower.

c. Reduced prices among retailers through the healthy competition they furnish.

d. The cash-and-carry field helps the individual buyer to keep close watch on the family budget.

e. System of chain store distribution fills need created by new era of mass production and rapid transportation.

f. They have desirable influence on social status of country as a whole.

g. Improve general social status of individual community.

X

IS THE LOCAL MERCHANT DOOMED?

106

Two of the most important questions mentioned are those
concerning the supposed doom of the local merchant as a result of chain-store development and the taxation problem of
the chain stores. First, let us look at the question involving the supposed doom of the independent dealer. The following report will clarify the situation; it is taken from the
authority of Paul C. Olsen, Ph.D.

Are present day competitive conditions driving individual retailers out of business? Are those fewer opportunities for individuals to go into business for themselves?
These cuestions are answered vehemently in the affirmative
by energetic advocates who today espouse the cause of the
local merchant.

Opponents of such conclusions do not deny that local
merchants today are going out of business in large numbers,
but they say that local merchants always have gone out of
business in large numbers. They also say that the number
and proportion of such local merchants going out of business
today is no larger than it was years ago when competitive
conditions were vastly different than they are now.

The purpose of this investigation has been to get the
facts which would support one or the other of these opposing
points of view. Texarkana, Texas, and the adjoining city
of the same name in Arkansas, is the place in which this investigation has been made. Food stores were chosen because
this is a class of retail stores from which complaints in

recent years of oppressive competitive conditions have been greater than those from any other kind of retailers.

Fourteen per cent of the individually owned food stores in business in Texarkana in January 1935, had gone out of business by the time listings were made in January, 1936; fourteen per cent is the lowest figure for any but one of the eleven immediately preceding years, as the following table shows.

PERCENTAGE OF INDIVIDUAL FOOD STORES GOING OUT OF BUSINESS

EACH YEAR FROM 1925 to 1936

TABLE NO.1

1925	20%
1926	22
1927	36
1928	17
1929	21
1930	25
1931	7
1932	35
1933	31
1934	28
1935	27
1936	14

Average for twelve years 22%

Present day complaints of difficult competitive conditions for individually owned food stores have existed all

through the twelve years included in Table No. 1. Therefore it is of interest to know whether or not in this same
city under competitive conditions different from these complained of during the past twelve years, the proportionate
number of individual food retailers going out of business
was less than in these t,elve recent years. In the table
below the facts are shown for the twelve years from 1901 to
1912.

PERCENTAGE OF INDIVIDUAL FOOD STORES GOING OUT OF BUSINESS

EACH YEAR FROM 1901 to 1912

TABLE NO. 2

Year	Percentage
1901	25%
1902	17
1903	15
1904	56
1905	29
1906	33
1907	40
1908	40
1909	34
1910	33
1911	17
1912	30

Average for twelve years 30%

109

There are other facts about the individual food stores in Texarkana which can be used to form a judgment about the effect upon them of the competitive conditions complained of in recent years. If these competitive conditions decrease the opportunity for individuals to go into business for themselves, there would be a marked decrease in the number of iddividual food stores started in Texarkana between 1925 and 1936. Of these four hundred and twelve new enterprises, two hundred and five, or almost exactly half, were started in the last six years, from 1931 to 1936. The proportionate number of individual food stores starting business each year in relation to the total number of individual food stores in business that year is shown in the following table:

PERCENTAGE OF INDIVIDUAL FOOD STORES STARTING BUSINESS EACH
YEAR FROM 1925 to 1936
TABLE NO. 3

1925	21%
1926	24
1927	24
1928	30
1929	24
1930	27
1931	8
1932	22
1933	36
1934	38
1935	22

110

While the figures in this table show the apparent attractiveness which individual ownership of a food store holds
to persons starting business in this field, in recent years,
it is important to compare this apparent attractiveness of
the recent years with that existing in years in which today's
advocates of the independent store owner say competitive conditions were vastly more favorable to the individual store
proprietor.

It is true that the proportionate number of individual
food store proprietors going into business in the twelve
years between 1901 and 1912, was at a considerably higher
average rate than was the case between 1925 and 1936. This
is shown by a comparison of the figures in the table below
with those in the preceding table.

PERCENTAGE OF INDIVIDUAL FOOD STORES STARTING BUSINESS EACH

YEAR FROM 1901 to 1912

1901	30%	1907	29%
1902	27	1908	25
1903	61	1909	33
1904	35	1910	43
1905	46	1911	27
1906	43	1912	33

Average for twelve

years 35%

111

Lest it be felt that the higher proportionate number
of individual food store proprietors who entered into
business between 1901 and 1912, is conclusive evidence of
the greater opportunity to start such enterprises then,
the figures in Tables number one and two, showing the proportionate number of individual food stores going out of
business in both twelve year periods should be compared.
Such a comparison shows that the proportionate number of
individual food stores going out of business each year
between 1901 and 1912 averaged over thirty-six per cent
higher than it did between 1925 and 1936!

Thus mere entrance into the business of food retailing is no assurance of long continued success in it.
This assertion is substantiated by a comparison for the
two periods covered by this study of the proportionate
number of individual food stores started in Texarkana,
which remained in business only long enough to be listed
in one year.

Of the three hundred and forty-one individual food
stores started in Texarkana between 1901 and 1911, one
hundred and fifty-six, or forty-six per cent went out
of business in one year. The corresponding figures for
the years between 1925 and 1935, on the three hundred and
forty eight stores started in that time is one hundred and
forty three, or thirty seven per cent. Startlingly large
as it is, in both periods, the number of individual food

stores going out of business within one year after opening,
the fact is that the number of such quick retirements is
only four-fifths as large between 1925 and 1935, as it was
between 1901 and 1911.   Year by year, results for the two
periods are shown in Table No. 5, which follows:

YEAR STORES WERE STARTED	NUMBER OF STORES STARTED	NUMBER GOING OUT OF BUSINESS WITHIN ONE YEAR	PERCENT GOING OUT OF BUSINESS WITHIN ONE YEAR
1901	16	3	19%
1902	16	7	44
1903	47	31	55
1904	27	12	44
1905	42	22	52
1906	44	22	50
1907	27	22	44
1908	20	6	30
1909	26	11	42
1910	39	13	45
1911	27	17	63
TOTAL FOR ABOVE ELEVEN YEARS	341	156	46%

The second half of Table No. 5 will be found on page 113.

113

Table No. 5 continued

YEAR STORES WERE STARTED.	NUMBER OF STORES STARTED	NUMBER GOING OUT OF BUSINESS WITHIN ONE YEAR	PERCENT GOING OUT OF BUSINESS WITHIN ONE YEAR
1925	28	11	39%
1926	32	12	37
1927	30	7	23
1928	43	15	35
1929	35	14	40
1930	39	3	8
1931	12	9	75
1932	29	17	59
1933	50	24	48
1934	58	21	16
1935	32	10	31
TOTAL FOR ABOVE ELEVEN YEARS	388	143	37%

It may be suggested that many of the retirements from
the business of operating individual food stores in Texarkana resulted in the earlier years (1901 to 1911) from voluntary withdrawals due to the proprietor's accumulation of
competences, while in the latter years (1925 to 1935) these
retirements were involuntary and due to changed competitive
conditions. The fact is that between 1901 and 1911, ninety-
three per cent of the individual food stores started had
passed out of existence or to new owners within nine years.

114

The corresponding percentage for the years from 1925 to
1935 is ninety-one per cent. Details, year by year, are
shown in Table No. 6, below:

NUMBER OF YEARS INDIVIDUALLY OWNED FOOD STORES STAY IN
BUSINESS

	1901-11	1925-35
Out of business within one year	46%	37%
two years	66	54
three years	77	62
four years	83	71
five years	88	73
six years	89	78
seven years	90	82
eight years	92	84
nine years	93	91
Remaining in Business after nine years	7	9

Individually owned food stores have continued to be
numerically important in Texarkana--between 1900 and 1930,
the date of the latest population census, the population
of Texarkana increased one hundred and sixty-nine per cent
while the number of individual food stores increased one
hundred and ninety-four per cent. The number of these stores
in business each year appear in Table No. 7 on page 115.

115

NUMBER OF INDIVIDUALLY OWNED FOOD STORES IN BUSINESS EACH

YEAR

1900-1912			1924-1936	
1900	50		1924	133
1901	53		1925	134
1902	59		1926	136
1903	93		1927	122
1904	77		1928	141
1905	92		1929	145
1906	102		1930	147
1907	92		1931	149
1908	80		1932	132
1909	78		1933	139
1910	89		1934	154
1911	99		1935	147
1912	102		1936	150

Additional evidence that the economic importance of
individual food stores has been maintained in Texarkana
is provided by a comparison for the various census years
of the average population per individual ffod store. This
comparison has been made in Table No. 8, which follows:

POPULATION PER INDIVIDUALLY OWNED FOOD STORES IN TEXARKANA

1900	203
1910	174
1924	171*
1930	186

116

CONCLUSIONS

1. That in proportion to its population, Texarkana has just as many individually-owned food stores as it had ten, twenty-five, and thirty-five years ago.

2. That individually-owned food stores started in Texarkana between 1925 and 1935 have had a longer average life than did those started between 1901 and 1911.

3. That the rate at which the individual food stores of Texarkana have gone out of business in the last twelve years is lower than it was in a twelve-year period, twenty-five to thirty-five years ago.

4. That the higher rate at which individual food stores were started in Texarkana in a twelve-year period, twenty-five to thirty-five years ago (as compared with the last twelve years) is directly related through the correspondingly.higher rate at which the stores went out of business and shorter length of time that they stayed in business.

5. That the foregoing results of this Texarkana survey are made in agreement with the results of similar studies made on this subject in Fresno, Grand Rapids, Louisville, Mobile, Sacramento, Schenectady, and Wichita.

6. That in all of these widely scattered localities, for the period and for the type of store surveyed, there is no evidence that the local merchant is doomed!

XI

CHAIN STORE TAXATION --

ROBINSON-PATMAN ACT

THE ROBINSON-PATMAN ACT

REASONS FOR ENACTMENT.--The Seventy-fourth Congress witnessed several attempts to amend the Clayton Act in the interest of the small-scale distributor. This manifestation of concern for the local retailer was stimulated by three distinct factors. The first and foremost was the desire of Congress to curb or eliminate some of the abuses of which chains have been accused (and found guilty in many instances) in order to minimize their competitive advantage when secured through unfair means. Impressed by the seeming injustice of the disclosures of the Patman Investigation and urged on by those who had considerable at stake, Congress passed the bill in the closing days of the session.

A second reason for the passage of the Robinson-Patman Act at that time was that it was a crystalization of a growing sentiment against "big business." It had become increasingly popular to lay the blame for our economic ills on chain stores and other forms of big business, and here was an opportunity to demonstrate disapproval of the so-called growing "evil." The opponents of bigness were growing apprehensive lest the business and industrial leviathans get out of hand and destroy the millions of independent entrepreneurs, and here was an opportunity to check that tendency. This sentiment was voiced by President Franklin D. Roosevelt when, in a message to Congress on June 19, 1935, pertaining to tax methods and policies,

he declared "size begets monopoly" and that "without such
small enterprises our competitive economic society would
cease."

The third factor that apparently led to the passage
of this law was the widely held belief among independent
distributors that the National Industrial Recovery Act with
its codes of fair competition had been highly beneficial
to them since it had attempted to restrain certain aspects
of competition which were deemed repugnant to smaller business men. Wholesalers, especially, felt the need for something to replace the codes and they seized upon the Robinson-Patman Act as a partial substitute.

PROVISIONS OF THE ACT.--This act is at once an amendment to the Clayton Act, and an entirely new law. Section
one, which amends the Clayton Act, makes it unlawful for
sellers to discriminate in price between different buyers
of like grade and quality where the effect of such discrimination may be substantially to lessen competition, to tend
to create a monopoly, to injure, destroy, or prevent competition, with any person who grants or knowingly receives
the benefit of such discrimination or with customers of
either of them.

Certain defenses under the law are set up by this
section. If the price differentials make only due allowances for differences in cost, including cost of manufacture,
sales, and delivery for varying quantities, they are not

discriminatory, except that the Federal Trade Commission
may determine quantity limits where it finds that available
large-scaler purchasers are so few as to render quantity
price differentials unjustly discriminatory or promotive
of monopoly. Under such conditions. quantity price differentials must be limited to such differentials as the
Federal Trade Commission shall prescribe.

The amendment to the Clayton Act permits the selection
of customers where done in good faith and when not in re-
straint of trade. It permits price changes under certain
specified conditions to meet market fluctuations, to dis-
pose of perishables, to avoid obsolescence of seasonal
goods; it permits distress sales under court order, and
bona fide closing-out sales. If, however, anyone feels
that he is the victim of discrimination in price, serives,
or facilities furnished, he may enter a complaint. If
proof of such discrimination is given at a hearing or
otherwise obtained by the Commission, the burden of jus-
tifying the deviations rests with the accused, and he
must refute the testimony against him, or the Commission
may order the discrimination stopped. He may allege that
tne so-called "discrimination" was made in good faith to
meet competition; that the transactions were intrastate
rather than interstate commerce; that the price differentials were the result of variations in actual costs; that
the goods in dispute were sold for export; or that services
and not goods were the subject of sale.

120

The act further attempts to outlaw the practice of
giving brokerage payments to a so-called agent, who actually works for a buyer under the latter's control re-
gardless of the services actually performed. A broker
may only collect a commission when he acts as a bona fide
third party. If he serves as a representative of the seller
to locate buyers, or as a representative of the buyer to find
sources of supply, and is really in business for himself,
he is discharging the true functions of a broker, insofar
as the vendor is concerned, and may be properly compensated.
When one acts, however, for or under the control of the
buyer he is not a true broker and no seller can be expected
to pay this intermediary for such service. Furthermore,
according to the first officials' interpretation of this
provision of the law issued on June 5, 1937, by the Federal Trade Commission attorneys, the law prohibits "payment
of brokerage fees from sellers to buyers directly or in-
directly.W This means that even an independent broker is
not entitled to any fee from a vendor if all or part of
it is passed back to the buyer, as was done by the Biddle
Purchasing Company and some others. It is on this ground
that this company was ordered to cease and disist from
such practices through order of the Commission. The com-
pensation must be primarily for services rendered to the
seller although the buyer may also benefit therefrom, but
not in a monetary way.

121

Advertising allowances to selected customers are also attacked by the Robinson-Patman Act. In the words of the act, it is "unlawful...to make any payment...to...a .....customer...in consideration for any services...unless such payment...is available on proportionally equal terms to all other customers competing in the distribution of such products. In other words, it becomes unlawful to offer advertising allowances as subterfuges for special price concessions. If they are made available to one buyer, the seller has to offer them to all on "proportionally equal terms."

Discrimination between purchasers is further restricted by requiring sellers to offer services or facilities for producing, handling, or selling to all buyers on substantially the same terms. And what is more, it is not only unlawful for the seller to discriminate in favor of certain buyers but it is also contrary to law for a business man knowingly to induce or receive a discrimination in price which is prohibited by any of the provisions heretofore mentioned. The buyer as well as the seller becomes guilty under the provisions of this act.

The Robinson-Patman Act not only amended the Clayton Act, but it also introduced several new provisions into Federal legislation, pertaining to marketing. Specifically, the act contains three sections of new law. The procedure for the Federal Trade Commission on cases pending or in process under the original Clayton Act is specified in the

7

in the first section of the new law. The second section
exempts cooperative associations from penalities under the
act for returning patronage dividends to members, although
in all other respects the law applies to cooperatives as to
other types of business. The third section contains the
following three provisions, which, overlapping in part the
provisions of the amended Clayton Act, confuse the meaning
of the new law:

1. It is unlawful to discriminate by giving discounts
rebates, allowances, or advertising-service charges to one
purchaser which are not accorded to competitors who buy a
like grade, quality and quantity.

2. It is unlawful to sell in one part of the country
in order to destroy competition or to eliminate a competitor by granting lower prices than those exacted elsewhere
in the United States.

3. It is unlawful to sell at unreasonable low prices
to destroy competiton or to eliminate a competitor.

For violation, a penalty of five thousand dollars
fine, imprisonment of not more than one year, or both is
provided by this part of the act, thus making it a crimi-
nal statute.

EFFECT OF THE ROBINSON-PATMAN ACT ON CHAINS.--The im-
mediate effect of the passage of the new law was psycholog-
ical; it frightened business men. It gave them what many
called "The Robinson-Patman jitters." Rather than be cited

under the act, many producers discounted discounts that
they feared might be labeled discriminatory. The instinc-
tive desire to avoid violating any legal mandate drove
numerous buyers and sellers to cover. The law focused
attention on certain prevalent abuses. Fear, however, was
not the only motive that made sellers refrain from granting
excessive discounts to large buyers. Many manufacturers
seized upon the new law as an excuse for discontinuing
certain unprofitable price policies. The act was a con-
venient alibi for taking a step that many sellers had heretofore lacked the courage to take.

A more lasting effect of the law on business is that
concerning manufacturer's price structures. There is little doubt but that the manufactuers' prices will be revised
and usually to the detriment of the chains and other large
buyers, including among them some of the large wholesalers
and voluntary chains that buy through centralized purchasing offices. In many cases the discounts given to large
purchasers were much greater than the economies effected as
a result of the large volume of business or quantity bought.
But in some instances, the Robinson-Patman Act may serve
as a boomerang for the small buyers who so enthusiastically
urged its passage. Careful analysis of differences in the
cost of manufacture, handling, and selling when dealing with
chains may show that the latter do not receive so large a
price differential as the resulting economies justify.

124

One effect that will very definitely work to the detriment of chains is that many manufacturers will dispense with allowances altogether in preference to attempting to offer them to all customers on <u>proportionally equal terms</u>. In many cases, the difficulties in attempting to apportion allowances among small as well as large buyers will make their use impossible. For example, if an advertising allowance of eight dollars per one hundred cases is offered to chain stores, what should the manufacturer offer the small retailer who buys but one case? Obviously, with the resulting eight cents, one can see that such an allowance would buy little in the way of advertising. The obstacles in the path of legal application of allowances will force many to abandon their use entirely, as has already been done in a number of cases.

In order to circumvent these disadvantages, it is very probable that chains may enter into agreements with producers to buy every thing they put out. In such an event, there is but one customer serviced by a manufacturer, hence, there can be no question of price discrimination. Likewise, it is probably that some manufacturers will choose to sell only to chains and other larger buyers, and as long as each is offered substantially the same price the element of discrimination is not a factor. Some chain organizations are already following the above practices. From the standpoint of the manufacturer, this appears to be a very dangerous procedure as he limits himself to one or a very few outlets.

125

He is in a position to be squeezed out by the chains for
lower prices, and he may ultimately be scueezed out of
business altogether. At any rate, by restricting his outlets the manufacturer places himself entirely at the mercy
of these customers.

Although this new act has been in effect only a comparatively short time, a very noticeable trend toward the
use of private brands has already become evident. Large
buyers find it more profitable to push their own brands
rather than to promote the sale of merchandise bearing the
manufacturer's label. An inspection of the shevles of almost any large chain grocery store is likely to show a
considerable quantity of privately branded merchandise.
The trend toward private brands is not entirely traceable
directly to the Robinson-Patman Act since the tendency was
very definitely in that direction before the law was enacted. Other recent legislation, especially the fiir trade
laws tends to produce the same effect. It is true, however,
that the Federal law accentuated the movement toward private
brands.

As it becomes increasingly difficult to buy national
brands advantageously, there is likely to be a tnedency
for chain systdms to engage more extensively in manufacturing.
Some already are processing their oen goods, and, in view of
the limitations placed upon chains by the Robinson-Patman

126

Act and other recent legislation, the movement is sure to
gain momentum. The net result may be that chains will ex-
ercise even greater influence on our economic life by controlling a large share not only of the distribution of goods
but of the production as well.

A further result of the new law is that it will de-
prive chain systems of brokerage fees and commissions
which some of them have been in the habit of collecting
through "bogus" brokers. Only independent brokerage firms
established by a number of grocery chains, are not entitled
to charge sellers for facilitating distribution. In the
eyes of the law, these organizations are formed for the
purpose of "gleaning unearned fees." The chains which
formed Procon attempted to circumvent the law by claiming
exemption under the name of a cooperative enterprise.
The Federal Trade Commission maintained, however, that in
fact Procon was not a cooperative but a subterfuge for ex-
acting fees from sellers while acting in the capacity of
the buyer's agent. In the spring of 1937, the organization
was dissolved before a judicial decision could be secured,
but in view of the attitude of the Commission and the word-
ing of the law, there appears to be little doubt but that
brokerage organizations of this type will be banned.

SUMMARY

When chain stores started to expand, the independent
merchant found himself left behind in the wake of progress.
Soon, however, the independent merchant awoke to the fact
that he must get in line with the period of development. By
adopting better policies and methods, the superior independent merchants were able to compete with chain stores, thus
presenting a different outlook than was had at the outset of
chain store expansion.

Cooperative buying organizations, voluntary chains, and
supermarkets are counter-balancing the progress and advantages
of the chain store systems.

Legislation has assumed the role of the "mailed fist"
in curtailing chain store activities and expansion. The
Robinson-Patman Law is one of the newest legislations to
be enacted, and it makes it harder for chains to get the
same special discounts and allowances they could secure
before. The legislation of fair-trade laws may soon make
it hard for the chain stores to undersell independents on
nationally branded items. The biggest gun of the chain
store, the price weapon, is slowly being silenced, making
it easier for the modern independent to compete with the
chain store.

The future chain store expansion will be slowed up because of the expense involved. Chain stores have expanded
in the past by reinvesting their earnings. New legislation

taxes reinvested earnings at a higher rate than earnings
paid out in dividends, and thus, stockholders will demand
cash dividends which will limit the desire for expansion.

BIBLIOGRAPHY

The following are the sources from which I received
my information on chain stores. Due to the fact that
there are relatively few books that have been written
recently on the subject, I have been forced to confine
myself to the few that have, in order to present the
most up-to-date account possible.

Chain Store Distribution and Management----------Baxter

Chain Store Debate Manual------------------------Buehler

The Chain Store Problem--------------------------Beckman

Chain Store Manual-------------------------------Nichols

Report of Federal Trade Commission---------------1936

Is the Local Merchant Doomed?--------------------Olsen

Census of Business 1935--------------------------Vol. IV

Lightning Source UK Ltd.
Milton Keynes UK
UKHW021656021218
333216UK00012B/1490/P